NEW · MASTERS *of*

WOODTURNING

EXPANDING THE BOUNDARIES OF WOOD ART

NEW · MASTERS of WOODTURNING

EXPANDING THE BOUNDARIES OF WOOD ART

TERRY MARTIN & KEVIN WALLACE

Fox
Chapel Publishing

1970 Broad Street • East Petersburg, PA 17520
www.FoxChapelPublishing.com

ALAN GIAGNOCAVO
President

J. MCCRARY
Publisher

PEG COUCH
Acquisition Editor

JOHN KELSEY
PAUL HAMBKE
Editors

TROY THORNE
Creative Direction

LINDSAY HESS
Design

DEDICATION

This book is dedicated to the memory of Dona Z. Meilach,
who saw wood art for what it was before any of us.

© 2008 by Fox Chapel Publishing Company, Inc.
New Masters of Woodturning is an original work, first published in 2008
by Fox Chapel Publishing Company, Inc.

ISBN 978-1-56523-375-1 (cloth); 978-1-56523-334-8 (pbk.)

Publisher's Cataloging-in-Publication Data

Martin, Terry, 1947-

    New masters of woodturning : expanding the boundaries of wood art
/ Terry Martin & Kevin Wallace. -- East Petersburg, PA : Fox Chapel
Publishing, c2008.

       p. : ill. ; cm.

      ISBN: 978-1-56523-375-1 (cloth) ; 978-1-56523-334-8 (pbk.)

      1. Woodworkers--Biography. 2. Turning--Technique.
3. Woodwork. I. Wallace, Kevin. II. Title.

TT201 .M37 2008
684.08/3--dc22   0806

To learn more about the other great books from

Fox Chapel Publishing, or to find a retailer near you,

call toll-free 800-457-9112 or visit us at *www.FoxChapelPublishing.com*.

Note to Authors: We are always looking for talented

authors to write new books in our area of woodworking, design,

and related crafts. Please send a brief letter describing your idea to

Peg Couch, Acquisition Editor, 1970 Broad Street, East Petersburg, PA 17520.

Printed in China
10 9 8 7 6 5 4 3 2 1

ABOUT THE AUTHORS

Terry Martin is a wood artist, curator, and commentator on wood art. During the last twenty years, he has taken part in 80 exhibitions in seven countries and his work is part of many of the large private and public collections devoted to wood art. Martin was the author of *Wood Dreaming*, published in 1995, the only book ever produced on Australian woodturning. Martin has written more than 200 articles on wood art published in twelve journals in seven countries.

From 1999 to 2006, Martin was editor-in-chief of the woodturning journal *Turning Points*, the only journal dedicated solely to wood art. Martin also is a contributing editor to *Woodwork* magazine and writes for several other publications around the world. His greatest pleasure is writing about people he respects. Martin has written hundreds of articles dedicated to showing the world the amazing things people do with wood.

Kevin Wallace is an independent curator and writer, focusing on contemporary art in craft media. He has guest-curated exhibitions for the Los Angeles County Museum of Art; the Craft and Folk Art Museum, Los Angeles; the Long Beach Museum of Art; the Cultural Affairs Department of Los Angeles; Los Angeles International Airport; the San Luis Obispo Art Center; and the Beatrice Wood Center for the Arts. He has previously curated two exhibitions for the Long Beach Museum of Art: *Into The Woods* and *Transforming Vision: The Wood Sculpture of William Hunter, 1970-2005*.

Wallace is a member of the Board of Directors of *Collectors of Wood Art* and on the Advisory Board of the *Handweavers Guild of America*. He is a contributing editor for *American Woodturner* and *Shuttle, Spindle & Dyepot* and a regular contributor to *Craft Arts International* (Australia) and *Woodturning* Magazine (England), writing about contemporary art in craft media (wood, ceramic, and fiber) and wood artists. Wallace serves on the Board of Directors of *Collectors of Wood Art (CWA)* and on the Advisory Board of the *Handweavers Guild of America*.

Wallace is the author of seven previous books: *River of Destiny: The Life and Work of Binh Pho*, 2006; *Transforming Vision: The Wood Sculpture of William Hunter*, 2005; *The Art of Vivika and Otto Heino*, 2004; *Celebrating Nature–Craft Traditions/Contemporary Expressions*, 2003; *Contemporary Glass: Color, Light and Form,* (with Ray Leier and Jan Peters), 2001; *Baskets: Tradition & Beyond,* (with Leier and Peters), 2000, and *Contemporary Turned Wood: New Perspectives in a Rich Tradition,* (with Leier and Peters), 1999.

ABOUT *NEW MASTERS OF WOODTURNING*

Since Dale Nish wrote *Master Woodturners* (1986), the field of woodturning has grown immensely. The artists featured in *New Masters of Woodturning* create a range of technically and aesthetically challenging works that push the boundaries of craft and art. *New Masters of Woodturning* offers a unique, international perspective. The book brings together artists from countries where the field of creative turning has taken root. The artists share their personal motivations, thought processes, and studio techniques. The many photographs show them at home and in their studios, and illustrate many of the techniques they employ.

New Masters of Woodturning presents a wealth of approaches, techniques, and philosophies of woodturning.

The book explores the influence of other leading woodturners and offers a historical perspective. Many of the artists have been influenced by other disciplines, including architecture, sculpture, literature and indigenous art, as well as the ever-present power of nature.

The book will be of interest to every woodturner and others working in wood who have an interest in self-expression, sculpture and the decorative arts. The book will serve as an important document of turn-of-the-century arts and craft, bringing contemporary woodturning to a larger audience. As the book concerns thought and process, it will be of interest to artists in a range of media, as well as collectors of art and craft.

CONTENTS

COVER

J. Paul Fennell, *De la Mer* (Of the Sea), 2007. African sumac, 9" high x 11¼" diameter. For more of Fennell's work, see page 13. Photo courtesy the artist.

TITLE PAGE

Marc Ricourt, *Vessel*, 2005. Walnut, ferrous oxide, 25" x 9" diameter. Ricourt's work resembles rusted iron, or ancient pottery. For more of Ricourt's work, see page 169.

OPPOSITE

Louise Hibbert, *Salt and Pepper Mills*, collaboration with Sarah Parker-Eaton, 2003. English sycamore, silver, resin, acrylic inks, and ceramic mechanism. This set of salt and pepper mills is a fine example of production woodturning. For more of Hibbert's work, see page 145.

INTRODUCTION

Woodturning in the 21st Century

During the 1960s and '70s, turned wooden bowls first came to be considered as objects of contemplation rather than simply of function. An art-like market gradually developed among collectors who considered such bowls too beautiful to use. Turners of vision started to ignore tradition, and to make pieces that broke many of the old "rules" of the craft. It was a quiet revolution, but a strangely disconnected one, because many participants had no idea what the others were doing. If anyone read about woodturning, it would have been in books emphasizing the trade values of techniques, not of innovative shapes or aesthetics.

In 1976, the American writer Dona Z. Meilach first documented the work for what it was—the beginning of a new art movement. In her book, *Creating Small Wood Objects as Functional Sculpture*, Meilach assembled much previously scattered history and put it into a larger context. She was probably the first person to describe turning as "sculptural" and to refer to turners as "artists." Meilach also introduced people who would shape the new field, such as Melvin Lindquist, Bob Stocksdale and Canada's Stephen Hogbin (page x). Meilach's work alerted many artists to the fact that there were others like them, and also inspired many newcomers to join the movement. Meilach continued publishing

insightful books on the fields of wood art and general craft, more than 100 in all, until her death in late 2006.

During the 1970s and into the '80s, the then-new *Fine Woodworking* magazine published a series of articles that reached an enormous audience around the world and changed the future of turning forever. The series included stories on turning delicate bowls of exotic timber by Bob Stocksdale; heavily spalted wood, previously unheard of, by Mark Lindquist; green turning, a technique practiced by turners for hundreds of years, by Alan Stirt; inlaid wood with hi-tech finishes by Giles Gilson, and, most significant of all, a 1979 article by David Ellsworth (page xi) on hollow turning. Ellsworth laid down his challenge to the turning world: "Bowl turning is one of the oldest crafts. It is also among the least developed as a contemporary art form." Ellsworth was good at explaining the technical aspects of his work—lathe specifications, speed, tools—but he also introduced language and a philosophy that had never before been heard in relation to turning: "The concentration involves all senses equally, and the center of focus is transferred to the tip of the tool." It was heady stuff, just right for the times, and it hit the mark in a culture ready for rule-breakers.

In 1980, Dale Nish of Provo, Utah, published the milestone book *Artistic*

Ron Fleming, *Yama Yuri*, 2006. Basswood, acrylics; 36" high x 17" diameter. Fleming created the turned vase as a vehicle for the painted lilies, which are life-size. He says, "I had to reinvent the air-brush process to be able to apply the frisket on a curved surface. There's more than 400 hours in it." For more of Fleming's work, see page 31.

STEPHEN HOGBIN: BREAKING OUT OF ROUNDNESS

Stephen Hogbin was born and educated in England, then immigrated to Canada in 1968, to teach design. In 1974, he astonished the craft world with an audacious exhibition timed to coincide with a World Craft Congress meeting being held in Toronto that year. Hogbin was, perhaps more than any other person, responsible for upsetting the tyranny of the circular form that had dominated the turning world for thousands of years.

Hogbin's first book, *Woodturning: The Purpose of the Object*, was published in the mid-1970s and shattered many

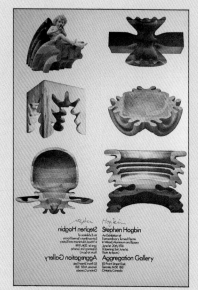

Stephen Hogbin's 1974 Toronto exhibition astounded woodturners and the larger craft world alike. As the woodturning writer and educator Mark Sfirri has said, "Hogbin was 20 years ahead of his time, and now, 30 years later, he is still 20 years ahead of his time."

preconceptions about materials and techniques. As Steven Kennard (page 139) said, "It really opened a door, as this idea was so new to me—that something which primarily makes round objects could be used to produce sculptural pieces that left you wondering how they were created." Hogbin showed the way for the many artists who would later cut, rejoin, color, combine materials, and bend the rules. Marilyn Campbell (page 133) said, simply, "He showed me turning could be art."

David Ellsworth, right, presents the American Association of Woodturners lifetime achievement award to Mark Lindquist, left, and Stephen Hogbin, center, at the AAW's 2007 conference. Photo by John Kelsey.

Woodturning. Nish showed foresight when he put the word artistic on the cover and he introduced ideas that profoundly influenced turners around the world. Nish spoke of paying "tribute to nature's designs," and of making the most of faults and damage in wood. Nish was one of the first to chronicle the changing ways turners were using wood, and their new approaches to displaying its beauty.

Nish followed up in 1985 with *Master Woodturners*, featuring the work of nine artists who, if they were not already, were transformed into turning icons: the Americans David Ellsworth, Mark Lindquist, Ed Moulthrop, Rude Osolnik, Al Stirt, and Jack Straka, along with England's Ray Key and Australia's Richard Raffan. The inclusion of the latter two was an early indication the new field was becoming an international phenomenon. In 1985, The Taunton Press published *Turning Wood*, the first of Raffan's widely sold series of how-to books and videos, which many artists today cite as a valuable part of their education.

Other turners who were repeatedly acknowledged as mentors and exemplars in interviews for this book include David Pye, Del Stubbs, Bob Stocksdale, Michael Hosaluk, Al Stirt, John Jordan, Jean-Francois Escoulen, and Mike Scott. It is impossible to give credit to all of those who deserve it, yet it is worthwhile mentioning the reputations of some woodturners have been compounded by repetition during the last thirty years, while many equally deserving names have been passed over. Like any field of endeavor, creative woodturning has a history filled with anonymous and forgotten contributors.

A New Collector

The new work attracted a new kind of collector, people who not only fell in love with the lure of wood, but also believed the leading woodturners could become the new art stars. It was not to be the case. If the new turning heroes became famous, it was not in the broader art field, but among the legion of aspiring turners with lathes in their garages who sought to create similar work. The amateur artisans formed a new market for tools and hardware, and for a time each new turning idea generated a new line of equipment. From sophisticated hollowing systems to ever-larger lathes, vast numbers of tools were manufactured and sold to the burgeoning amateur market. As a result, a thin and difficult-to-navigate line developed between amateurs who were able to create technically proficient work, largely by imitating or taking classes from their heroes, and those who had a distinctly original aesthetic vision that propelled the field forward.

Very early on, a small group of woodturners emerged as the collectible masters. The group included James Prestini, Bob Stocksdale, Melvin and Mark Lindquist, Rude Osolnik, and Ed Moulthrop. As the field expanded during the 1980s and '90s, new artists entered the gallery system, among them such innovators as Todd Hoyer, Stoney Lamar, Michael Peterson, Giles Gilson, John Jordan, Mike Scott, and Michelle Holzapfel. The infusion created challenges for new collectors and curators, who had to navigate a scene where accomplished artists exhibited alongside emergent novices. The early success of the

DAVID ELLSWORTH: HOLLOW LIKE AN EGGSHELL

Ellsworth came to broad notice in 1979 when *Fine Woodworking* magazine introduced his techniques for hollowing wood through narrow openings to create vessels more like pottery than any woodwork that had gone before. His work overturned all of the deeply held traditions of functionality that had defined turning. Ellsworth himself was profoundly influenced by Native American pottery, and he planted the seeds for the explosion of creative woodturning that was to follow. For the first time, woodturners were seeing themselves as artists.

David Ellsworth, *Ovoid Pot #1*, spalted sugar maple, 6" high x 11" diameter. His pieces combine the fluid lightness and elegant form of pottery with the beautiful figure and texture of wood.

Ellsworth went on to help found the American Association of Woodturners, serving several terms as its president. He continues to produce his astonishing hollow-turned turned vessels at his studio in Quakertown, Pennsylvania, where he also teaches weekend seminars and manufactures his own line of tools for hollow turning.

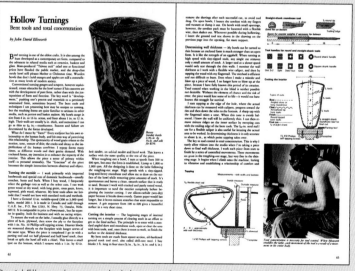

David Ellsworth astounded the woodworking world with his 1979 magazine account of his hollow-turning techniques, combined with his perspective on where his work fit in the larger craft/art world.

RICHARD RAFFAN: GOOD TECHNIQUE AND GOOD DESIGN

Many thousands of woodturners have learned basic skills by imitating Richard Raffan, via his many books, videos, and DVDs.

Richard Raffan often is acknowledged for demystifying the very ancient craft of turning, showing how almost anyone could achieve superb results using simple tools and techniques. A turner since 1970, Raffan published the first of his series of how-to books, *Turning Wood with Richard Raffan* (Taunton Press), in 1985. Since then, he has traveled tirelessly as a demonstrator and teacher, in the process emigrating from England to Eastern Australia. He is perhaps the person most responsible for spreading the idea that anyone can learn to turn wood. Raffan always has emphasized the need for good line and simplicity of design, and recognizes the generations of British production turners who went before him. In his own words, "I don't feel the need to be different, but I would like to be good." As the German turner Peter Hromek (page 37) said, "I found a translation of Richard Raffan's book on woodturning design and it became my bible."

Richard Raffan, *Bowl* (production work). Oak, 16" diameter. Raffan's appeal lies in his no-nonsense combination of professionally efficient techniques with an excellent, and explainable, sense of design. Photo courtesy the artist.

true innovators suggested originality was the key to sales, so the new generation began to create ever more unusual and technically complex work. At the same time, some who had already made their mark by creating original work seemed condemned to repeat their ideas incessantly, to satisfy the desire of collectors to own a signature piece.

Round No More

Woodturning is unlike other traditional woodcrafts. In carving, furniture making, and carpentry, one takes pains to hold the wood still so it can be worked by moving tools. In woodturning, the lathe rotates the wood itself against a hand-guided tool. The inversion has two valuable consequences: much turned work can be completed right on the lathe with no additional processing, and woodturning offers a very quick path from fallen tree to finished object. It also brings a limitation formerly seen as inviolate: turned work is round.

Much of the wood art in this book inverts those truisms: the lathe is merely the beginning, with additional off-lathe processing to come. It is not at all quick, and it no longer has to be round.

Most of the early innovators made their work entirely on the lathe and the artists in the book generally started out doing the same. Most of them spent many years mastering the traditional skills of turning before feeling the need to add other techniques. Many don't use the lathe nearly as much now, and some struggle with whether they are "turners" at all. A piece of wood might spend a very brief time on the lathe, followed by months of reworking, sometimes removing or concealing any evidence it was initially turned. The trend in turned wood art now is to carve, burn, paint, recut, and rework pieces.

Once woodturning was valued for how quickly and inexpensively it could be done, but now artists boast of how many months they spend reworking a piece after turning it. However, many say their work is still "defined by the lathe" and most admit to a deep-seated love of the very ancient craft of turning. It is true that even when a piece has been reworked extensively, its beginnings as a round and symmetrical shape still will show through—its lines are too powerful to entirely disguise. The artists' loyalty to the lathe may seem surprising, however, because it is the work they do after turning that makes their work distinctly their own.

Perhaps the contradictions of turned wood art are best summarized by Vaughn Richmond (page 51) when he says, "Some of my woodturning may have an element of sculpture, and some of my sculptures may have an element of woodturning." At the same time, many wood artists simply define their work as turning. Hans Weissflog (page 63), the only turner in this book to have completed a traditional turning apprenticeship, is in no doubt about the importance of the lathe: "I believe the lathe provides more possibilities than most people know. That's what I want to show in my designs, as it is my most important tool."

The beauty of wood is what attracts many artists in the first place, and much early work celebrates it. It is about the wood's appearance, smell, grain, texture, and links with the natural world. In the early days,

Photo by Grant Kernan

Photo courtesy the artist

ABOVE

Michael Hosaluk's colors are much admired. See page 75.

LEFT

Binh Pho's work is unbelievably intricate. See page 163.

a clever use of wood grain was enough to claim artistry. Even now, when artists may obscure the wood by texturing, burning, and painting, it still has appeal in its warmth, heft, and vitality. Christophe Nancey (page 103) puts it well: "I see the wood as my first tool and my first source of inspiration."

For many of the artists in this book, their immediate environment is another important part of who they are and what they create, and pursuing a solitary craft with an uncertain income is their method for being able to live in places they love.

Exciting New Techniques

For a long time, many who were promoting wood art liked to compare it to ceramics and art glass. They were looking for a vocabulary to help build credibility in the top-end market. In reality, contemporary wood art uses techniques as exciting as anything being done in other fields. Burning the wood has progressed from rough blowtorching to refined finishing and patterning, such as the delicate burnt textures of Graeme Priddle (page 157). Texturing has expanded to include everything from the controlled brutality of Marc Ricourt's slashed finishes (pages ii and 169) to the delicacy of carved surfaces by Jacques Vesery (page 69) or Liam Flynn (page 1). Where painting and color once were treated with suspicion, the playful use of color by Michael Hosaluk (page 75) and others now is much admired. Much of Ron Fleming's work depends upon his skills as an illustrator (pages viii and 31), while Binh Pho's pieces (page 163) are more about color and carving than anyone in the early days could have imagined. Once wood was the sacrosanct material, but now it's complemented by other materials, such as

the spun metal of William Moore (page 45). If anyone doubts turned wood art is now as much about carving, texturing, and sanding as it is about turning, they only have to look at the astonishing work of Alain Mailland (page 181). One day, wood art will be recognized for the repertoire of techniques and processes it has fostered.

While turned wood art has its roots in utility, today's artists often encounter a prejudice against function. Galleries, collectors, and museum curators tend to frown upon production work and functional bowls, suggesting those woodturners

RIGHT

William Moore mates metal and wood. Detail, *Equilibrium*, see page 45.

BELOW LEFT

Liam Flynn repeats fine patterns across subtly figured wood. Detail, *Untitled* (2006), see page 2.

BELOW RIGHT

Jacques Vesery carves and paints tiny, delicate creatures. See page 69.

Photo by Dan Kvitka

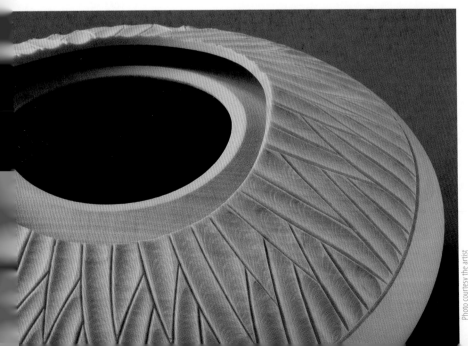

Photo courtesy the artist

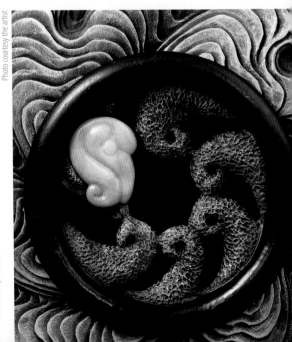

Photo courtesy the artist

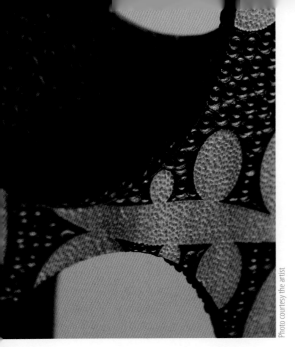

Photo courtesy the artist

By featuring the work of fourteen Americans, two Australians, three Canadians, one Irishman, two New Zealanders, one South African, four Frenchmen, two Germans, and two Britons, this book shows the international flavor of the contemporary turning movement. The turning renaissance coincided with the rise of the Internet and niche publications, so more information about new ideas and techniques probably has been exchanged during the last twenty years than in the previous 2,000 years. The popularity of seminars and club demonstrations has increased exponentially and now some turners travel internationally for much of each year in the northern and southern hemispheres, teaching, demonstrating, and acting as turning ambassadors.

The authors are responsible for choosing the artists represented here, but after that, we have tried to let the artists speak for themselves. It is their world and they know it best. One inspiring aspect of their world has been the willingness of everyone to share their ideas, techniques, and joy in what they do. While there are distinct differences in how people work, there are no trade secrets. We are fortunate the woodturners in this book have shared their lives so freely with us and our sincere thanks go out to them.

— *Terry Martin, Brisbane, Australia, and Kevin Wallace, Los Angeles, CA.*

LEFT

Graeme Priddle patterns the wood by charring it. Detail, *Tahi Rua* (One Two), see page 157.

will not be accepted as "serious artists." However, many woodturners continue to produce functional multiples as a means of supporting their families and because they simply enjoy the work. Louise Hibbert (pages vi and 145) believes utilitarian work still is important. "Repeating forms keeps my turning skills up to speed," she says. "I love my living environment to be filled with useful things, hand made with care and filled with personal significance. Its a sad fact that hand-made functional items, imbued with individuality, are seen as less valuable than sculptural pieces."

From ancient and humble beginnings, woodturning has been transformed into an art form for the twenty-first century. As both wood and fine craftsmanship become more precious in a machine-made world, the art not only reminds us of a simpler past, but it also shows nothing is fixed and old skills can evolve unexpectedly. The artists in this book acknowledge their predecessors, both ancient and more recent. In turn, we hope the work in these pages will inspire others to grow in new directions.

LIAM FLYNN

Striving to Find the Perfect Line

Woodturning has a venerable history in Ireland, where the oldest finds of turned wooden bowls date back around 2,000 years. For most of that time, the wares made on the lathe were traditional functional items, such as bowls and ladles.

Liam Flynn is a modern Irish turner in every sense, including his use of traditional oak for many of his projects. Unlike his predecessors, though, Flynn designs his work not to be used. Once he has ebonized the finished work, it has a deep patina that evokes ancient vessels blackened by their long slumber in the peat bog of archaeological sites.

Flynn's plans for his life didn't initially include becoming a turner, though a future in woodworking always was likely. "My family has been involved in

---

I dislike 'stunning wood grain' in the traditional sense. I prefer a plain canvas.

---

woodworking for generations. I was working with wood as far back as I can remember and I started out making very basic furniture," he explains.

Flynn finds it hard to remember exactly why he became a turner. "It's kind of difficult to find a reason—It just happened!" He explains that in 1982, he purchased John Makepeace's *The Woodwork Book*, which featured woodturners Richard Raffan (page xii) and Bob Stocksdale. Flynn was very taken by their work. "It was my first introduction to what was possible on the

Photo by Brendan Leahy

ABOVE

Shavings fly off the unseasoned wet wood like peelings from a ripe apple. The wood is soft, almost malleable, and yields quickly to Flynn's sharp tools.

OPPOSITE

Untitled, 2006. Ebonized oak; 13" high x 7½" diameter. A beautiful example of finely controlled surface carving. The shaped rim is more interesting than a straight rim.

lathe," Flynn says. The book also contained an essay entitled, "Making Your Work Your Own," by furniture maker James Krenov. "He got me thinking about, as he puts it, '...the fingerprints on the object of the person who

---

The distortion that takes place during the drying process is a significant part of my work.

---

made it.' I found I agreed with his belief that the process is so important."

Soon after David Ellsworth astonished the turning world with his hollow vessels (page xi), they became commonplace because of imitators. The fashion for surface decoration arose because vessel makers were trying to distinguish their work from the mass of look-alikes. However, a well-formed simple vase shape remains one of the most impressive things that can be produced wholly on the lathe. A few dedicated professionals have continued to devote themselves to such work, and Flynn is one of the best. His use of plain wood, usually blackened, means his shapes have to be perfect and he succeeds wonderfully. Also, when he decorates the surface of his vessels, it is not for the sake of novelty, but to enhance and emphasize the simple qualities of his elegant forms. Flynn is a modern master of the neo-classical wooden vessel.

ABOVE TOP

Untitled, 2006. Ebonized oak; 5" high x 9" diameter. The turned form is symmetrical but the surface carving is offset, giving the ebonized piece of oak a distinct character.

ABOVE BOTTOM

Still Life with Holly, 2007. Holly; 13½" wide. The delicately flaring bowl in white holly contrasts with the strongly enclosed form of its partner vessel. One is filled with light, the other with shadow.

OPPOSITE TOP

Untitled, 2006, Fumed oak; 7½" high x 10" diameter. Fuming with ammonia gives the piece its soft brown color, while allowing the rays in the wood to flash across the carved flutes.

OPPOSITE BOTTOM

Untitled, 2006. Holly; 6" diameter. The white holly wood in a delicate piece contrasts wonderfully with Flynn's ebonized pieces.

Photo by Brendan Leahy

Photo by Brendan Leahy

How Flynn Works

Flynn's work process starts with designing a piece while it is still part of the log. Flynn believes doing so is essential if he is to maintain control over the final shape the vessel will take, because he works in wet, unseasoned wood. As a result, the wood will shrink and move after Flynn is finished, so the way he cuts the piece in relation to the log's grain structure determines the eventual shape. Flynn says, "The distortion that takes place during the drying process is a significant part of my work." Flynn says he "tries to maintain a balance between the influence of the material and my input. I dislike 'stunning wood grain' in the traditional sense. I prefer a plain canvas." Flynn has been working as a turner long enough that technical challenges aren't problems any more. Also, he says, "I've learned my limitations and how to work within them. I've also learned there is no point in doing something just because it's difficult."

The materials Flynn chooses are commonly available where he lives. "I like to work with green oak. It has everything I want. It may not be the most attractive wood, but its other qualities make it irresistible for me and I only use wood that comes from renewable sources. I find the wood to be alive while I'm working it, really responsive. It's so easy to fashion it into the shapes I want. Even though I don't highlight the natural qualities of the material, such as the grain, the material is still central to my work."

ABOVE TOP

Flynn works the oak while it is wet and unseasoned. He says doing so makes it easier for him to work the wood the way he wants, though he must anticipate the shrinkage and distortion that will occur in the wood as it dries.

ABOVE BOTTOM

Half-completed pieces season gently in Flynn's rustic workshop. They're parked on every shelf and ceiling beam, and they fill the drying cabinet at center right.

Flynn chooses oak for other reasons too. "It's full of minerals, which make it ideal for fuming and ebonizing. I ebonize by painting on a solution of acetic acid and iron filings. The fuming is even easier—I simply suspend the piece in an airtight container and slip in a small saucer of industrial-grade ammonia. It's best to do the fuming outdoors as the fumes can be a little overwhelming. I find one hour's exposure to the ammonia fumes gives me the color change I seek."

Unlike many contemporary turners, Flynn believes the lathe defines his work. "All of my work is shaped on a lathe and is identifiable as woodturning. Sometimes 90 percent of the work spent on a piece is turning. The opposite has happened as well, especially on the intensively carved forms. I seem to keep returning to the same shapes, but they aren't the same. The challenge is to keep reinterpreting the forms. Sometimes minuscule adjustments can significantly alter a piece. I'm always striving to find the perfect line."

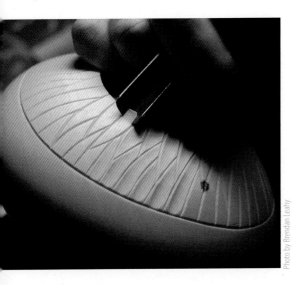

The wet wood yields easily to a sharp gouge and careful hands, creating the delicate finish Flynn requires.

The Soft Irish Countryside

Flynn lives in Abbeyfeale, a historic market town in County Limerick in the midwest of Ireland. He describes it with great affection: "The countryside consists of rolling green hills—soft would be a good description. The great thing about living in Ireland is if I drive a half hour west of here, I'm on the coast where the landscape is very different—all big jagged rocks. East of here it gets flatter and large trees are more common. The best thing about Abbeyfeale is the River Feale, which gives the town its name. The river flows through the town and is one of the top three salmon rivers in the country. It's my escape from the dust of the workshop. I'm there often, up to my waist in water, casting flies at some uninterested fish. The qualities required for salmon angling could be a metaphor for success in any walk of life—lots of patience, respect for our environment, diligent planning and, of course, the ability to handle disappointment."

Flynn's home includes a fairly large studio space and a large yard that used to be a builder's yard. He likes the generous space: "I can stockpile wood when I come across it and it gives me great freedom when I'm chain-sawing."

Flynn radiates a sense of contentment with what he does. "I want to continue what I'm doing and to retain the passion for it." Many of us could learn from Flynn's pride in his chosen career.

www.liamflynn.net

Flynn walks a country lane in the soft Irish landscape near his home.

HAYLEY SMITH

Ideas Evolve and Flow Into the Next Piece

Hayley Smith's experience as a painter and printmaker have led her to create works that marry the turned wood form with geometric fields of color and delicately carved surfaces. Smith's introduction to woodturning occurred during her second year at university in Britain. The students were required to explore various disciplines,

---

There is something wonderful about working while it is dark outside. When I enter my studio, it is like being enveloped in another world.

---

so she spent time in the ceramic department throwing pots, then moved into the metal and wood studios. Most students knew what they wanted to do there but, having no preference, Smith took the only equipment not being used—the wood lathe.

At the time, Smith viewed herself as a printmaker-painter, but in retrospect she realizes she enjoyed creating lino-cuts and wood blocks more than she enjoyed the resulting printed image. "I embraced working three-dimensionally and the subtractive process of woodturning," Smith says. "After working with clay, which is cold and wet, I enjoyed handling wood, which is a warm material. Wood brings its own character to the process, according to its species. It is challenging to work with initially, and I recognized the opportunity to bring to it elements from my past experience of painting and printmaking. I immediately used color and surface texture created

Photo by Ted Weller

ABOVE

Smith's completed pieces are painterly, but they all begin with her turning wood on the lathe.

OPPOSITE

Square Dance VI, 2003. Maple; 1¾" deep x 16¾" diameter. "An exploration of layered squares within circles, and circles within squares," Smith says.

ABOVE

Hemispherical Bowl #2/99. English sycamore; 3¼" height x 7¼" diameter. Smith worked with the hemispherical bowl form for a number of years. *Hemispherical Bowl #2* illustrates the development of deeper carved elements and the opening up of the form.

OPPOSITE

Square Dance VII, 2003. Maple; 2 ½" deep x 22" diameter. "*Square Dance VII* became the last Square Dance wall piece," Smith says. "The idea behind it was the cliché of a square peg not being able to fit into a round hole, and the small textured square can be seen drifting apart from the round central wood grain bowl."

both on and off the lathe in conjunction with the turned form."

Smith offers additional reasons as to why she enjoys working with wood. "I like the challenge of finding the balance between its existing character and what I can add to it. It is, after all, not a blank canvas. I spent several formative years trying to fight the very nature of the material, rather than yielding to it and working with it."

For Smith, the lathe defines her work because it is the starting point for each piece. It also serves as a discipline to work within, a framework similar to working on a canvas. Once the form has been created, Smith turns to her years of painting and printmaking.

It's Necessary to Make Art

When Smith married fellow woodturner Todd Hoyer, she left her home in Wales to reside with him in Bisbee, a former mining town turned artists' colony five miles north of the Mexican border in Southeastern Arizona. The couple found a place to build their home and studios a mile high in the Mule Mountains. The mountain ranges rise dramatically from the desert floor, resulting in eco-systems unlike everything around them. "The canyon is stunning," Smith says. "Ancient rock faces are sometimes lit up by the moon and at others by the sunset. They can be dusted with snow or running with waterfalls during the summer rains. Oaks, juniper, and pinyon pine are mixed with cactus, and the canyon is rich with wildlife, some of it not so harmless. The weather

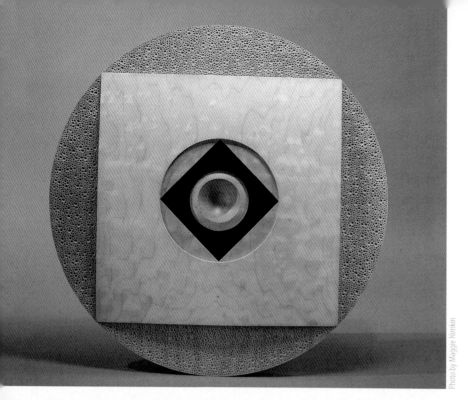

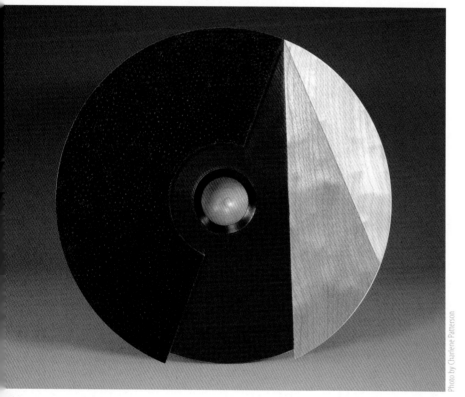

ABOVE TOP

Square Dance III, 2003. Maple, 2½" deep x 17½" diameter. "Sometimes a name leads to a piece, and sometimes a piece leads to a name," Smith says. "Out of all of the dances I explored, *Square Dance* led to one piece after another." Museum of Arts & Design, New York; gift of Robyn Horn.

ABOVE BOTTOM

War Dance, 2001. Maple; 1" deep x 9½" diameter. "I had a piece in progress the week of 9/11," Smith says. "It changed and became *War Dance*." Mobile Museum of Art, Mobile, Alabama, museum purchase with funds from an anonymous donor.

can be wild as well, with the temperature swinging 40 degrees in a day. The quality of the light is remarkable, the sky usually azure and the stars at night brilliant, not dimmed by city light pollution. The views from every window are inspiring." Smith says a love of the natural beauty of the world requires her to make art. "It is a necessary activity for me. I've always sought out places to work from in areas of great natural beauty."

"It is unproductive for me to work in my studio in the morning," Smith says of her average day. "The best working time for me is in the afternoon and I'm often my most creative in the evening. There is something wonderful about working while it is dark outside. To focus on my work, I need an organized space. I find mental clutter very distracting and I am easily distracted

Once I have an idea, the challenge is how to do it technically. Once I meet that challenge, I want to move on to the next idea and not repeat the process, but rather add to it.

by practical necessities, so I create an environment conducive to the way I work. When I enter my studio, it is like being enveloped in another world."

The wide-ranging artists who have influenced Smith include conceptual artist Andy Goldsworthy, sculptor Barbara Hepworth, ceramic artist Hans Coper, painter Piet Mondrian, and wood artists Jim Partridge and Maria Van Kesteren. Her work is idea-driven, and she spends a great deal of time drawing in her sketchbook and making intricate notes. Working with her sketchbook offers the opportunity to develop an idea, or for a new one to appear. "It's important to have a notebook, as I can't retain all of the ideas I have," she says. "Usually when I am working on a piece, ideas evolve and flow into the next piece."

While some artists work on several pieces simultaneously, Smith prefers to work on one piece at a time, so as not to dilute her focus. That makes the choice to pursue a particular idea important, because it is where she will be devoting all of her creative energy. "Once I have an idea, the challenge is usually how to bring the work to fruition technically. Once

Photo courtesy the artist

Photo courtesy the artist

I meet that challenge I want to move on to the next idea and not repeat the process, but rather add to it. I try to remain open and occasionally new ideas grow out of the technical aspects of my work."

Both Smith and Hoyer have had to take a break from creating their work to build their new home and studios. By the time Smith is able to get back to work, she will undoubtedly have all of the ideas she needs.

Photo courtesy the artist

J. PAUL FENNELL

Technical and Creative Challenges Are Always Mingled

Nearly all of J. Paul Fennell's work involves hollow forms. His earlier work focused on developing classical forms emphasizing the natural beauty of the material and the lathe was the dominant tool. Currently, Fennell is "interested in presenting an idea, feeling or emotion through my work, and how the observer responds to the piece. The pieces tend to be much more complicated in concept, form and surface decoration."

As his ideas have evolved, Fennell's reliance on the lathe also has evolved. "Although I use the lathe to create the hollow form, it has a lesser role now. The majority of time is spent on carving, piercing, texturing, and the like. A significant part of the work is the contemplation, planning, and laying out the design before work on the wood starts. The idea is to allow the rhythm of the pattern to express a theme or concept as it traverses the surface, in a visual and tactile language everyone can understand," Fennell explains.

"When I create a piece, there is the challenge of the design—a pattern, for example—being transformed from two dimensions onto the curved three-dimensional surface of a vessel. At other times, the challenge is taking an abstract concept or idea and interpreting it in a piece. In that way, my technical and creative challenges are always mingled," Fennell says.

All photos courtesy the artist unless otherwise indicated

ABOVE

"I often can acquire large (by desert standards) logs of mesquite, a very stable wood, and one of my favorites to turn," Fennell says.

OPPOSITE

View from the Bamboo Garden, 2006. African sumac; 11" high x 7" diameter. Fennell says, "I am fascinated with window lattice patterns typically found in China. In *View from the Bamboo Garden*, I employ a specific pattern—called ice ray or cracked ice—in a theme focusing on the importance of gardens in everyday life, places for solitary or social contemplation of nature."

LEFT

Fennell's layout pattern for *View from the Bamboo Garden* shows the bamboo motif and ice ray lattice patterns integrated together. Fennell creates his patterns by scanning images onto vinyl film.

BELOW TOP

"During the summer
monsoon, there is a
second rainy season,
and it is not uncommon
to experience full
ground-to-ground
rainbows such as this,"
Fennell says.

BELOW BOTTOM

"It is difficult not to
be awed and inspired,
waking up in the
morning to glorious
sunrises such as this,"
Fennell says.

Inspired by Mountains and Desert

Fennell believes he is fortunate to live and work on two acres in the northern reaches of the Sonoran desert in Scottsale, Arizona. "Contrary to a common perception about deserts, the Sonoran Desert has great biodiversity and the varied flora and fauna are well-adapted to the environment," Fennell says. "The surrounding mountains sometimes acquire a dusting of snow in the winter, but at any time of the year they change color during the day, from mauve and purple at sunup and sundown, to blue-gray silhouettes in the midday heat. We see full ground-to-ground rainbows during showers, as well as spectacular sunrises and sunsets." The native vegetation and surrounding mountains have been central to his work during the last decade.

Fennell has long been inspired by the fine arts. "Several artists have been major influences, sometimes in oblique ways. I always have been fascinated at how patterns are generated and pay homage to M.C. Escher because of his monumental efforts in this area. I admire the interplay

The recycled urban trees I get are mostly exotic species, giving me an opportunity to work with rare and beautiful woods that are not generally available.

of mathematics and art at which Escher excelled, especially his interlocking designs and distorted landscapes. Henri Matisse is also a favorite of mine, specifically in how he uses line and color as forms of expressiveness." Not surprisingly, Fennell's work is also inspired by the craft world. "David Pye impressed me with the importance of making things well. His comments about the diversity of design elements and how it influences the making and observation of work are especially relevant to me."

View from the Garden, 2006. African sumac, 7½" high x 6½" diameter. Fennell has portrayed a garden theme using three elements: the lattice, a textured wall, and the structure of tree branches. Each element is on a different level—the outermost is the tree, the next is the garden wall, the next is the lattice frame, and finally the lattice itself.

De la Mer (Of the Sea), 2007. African sumac, 9" high x 11¼" diameter. Carved and pierced, *De la Mer* is inspired by ocean waves and reflected light patterns on the ocean bottom, "from childhood memories when I lived on the East Coast, where the Atlantic Ocean was virtually the front yard of my home," Fennell says.

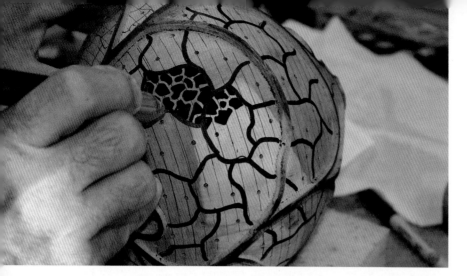

How Fennell Works: Pierced Walls

Of his introduction to woodturning, Fennell says, "Until the early 1970s, I had never been near a lathe. My first exposure was making a table with turned legs in an adult education workshop around 1971. After completing that project, I saw the lathe as a tool for more expressive work, but also a way to create utilitarian pieces very quickly compared to the time it took to make a piece of furniture."

Fennell enjoyed the technical challenges of teaching himself to use the lathe. He was unaware of the burgeoning field of artistic woodturning, but when he finally saw such artists as David Ellsworth (page xi), Frank Sudol, Bob Stockdale, Rude Osolnik, and Ed Moulthrop create work on the lathe in the 1980s, it was a revelation and he knew woodturning would become an important part of his life.

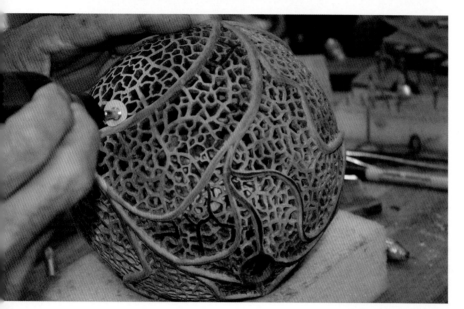

ABOVE TOP

In a process similar to relief carving on a thin-turned vessel, Fennell excavates between the leafy veins and pierces the wood using a power-carving tool.

ABOVE BOTTOM

With the carving and piercing completed, Fennell smoothes and refines the surfaces of the wood.

RIGHT

Leaf Form, 2005. African sumac; 8" high x 8" diameter. "I was fascinated as a youngster to watch beetles skeletonize leaves, leaving only the veins intact," Fennell says. "The background has to be relieved to achieve the effect of raised leaf veins, and the piercing mimics the beetles' handiwork."

Reverence for Wood

Wood and his reverence for it are perhaps Fennell's greatest inspiration. "I was exposed to wood as early as I can remember. I recall playing with scraps of wood as a toddler in my father's basement workshop," he says. "In junior high school, I enrolled in the woodshop classes and enjoyed them. I remember the pleasant smell of freshly cut or planed wood in a woodworking shop, and that may have contributed to the reverence I have for the material."

Finding wood in the desert is not always easy. "Generally, I don't rely on the commercial market for wood. No matter where you live, you can find many trees that are cut down and thrown away. The desert area does not support a lot of large indigenous trees and there are restrictions on the removal of them, even on private land. However, I live in a large urban area that does support many exotic species. They

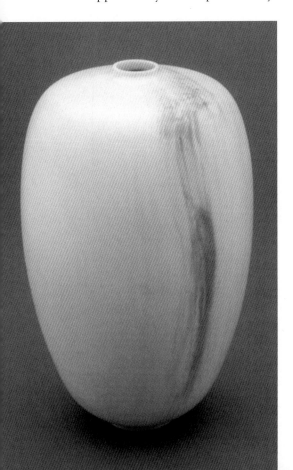

Photo by Abram's Photo/Graphics

have been introduced because of our mild climate. I am constantly on the lookout for such trees and have been successful. It means recycling a natural resource and remaining out of the loop of commercial exploitation and consumption of forest resources. An added benefit is the trees I get are mostly exotic species, giving me an opportunity to work with rare and beautiful woods that are not generally available."

Fennell explains why he likes to work with wood. "The material itself is easy to use in a home-shop environment and does not require the kind of expensive equipment needed for a ceramic or glass studio. With wood, forms can be developed, and changed, quickly. Lastly, the finished wood piece changes over time, developing a mellow, oxidized patina and gaining in stature as it matures."

www.jpaulfennell.com

ABOVE

Metallica Green, 1994. Citrus wood, metal leaf, lacquer; 8½" high x 5½" diameter. In the mid-1990s, Fennell developed his interest in surface decoration by applying metal leaf and lacquer on crisply turned wooden vessels. His current interest is in pierced and carved pieces.

LEFT

Subtlety, 1991. Bleached box elder, 9" high x 5½" diameter. Fennell's early work emphasized the natural beauty of the wood and the created beauty of the turned form, without carving and piercing.

HARVEY FEIN

Consider Texture, Pattern, and Inclusions

Harvey Fein is an inventor and artist who is "in love with the mechanics of things." A great deal of Fein's time goes into developing machinery to create the works he envisions.

Evidence of Fein's inventiveness rests with the four patents he holds and his design of countless minor projects and machines for his window shade business. "The idea for each came to me as a fully completed object," Fein says. "I worked backward in my head to figure out how to make it, then forward as I put it on paper. I'm in love with the mechanics of things. I need to know how things work. None of my childhood toys stayed whole for long and it is my great pleasure to fix all manner of broken machinery."

Only ten years have passed since a friend gave Fein a wood bowl he had made. "I had to know how he had done it. The minute he placed the gouge in my hand, I knew woodturning was for me and I bought my first lathe the same day." Fein went into the cellar

---

The minute he placed the gouge in my hand, I knew woodturning was for me and I bought my first lathe the same day.

---

with his new set of tools and books on turning, but soon realized a little personal coaching was in order. "I spent a weekend with David Ellsworth (page xi) and found him a very generous teacher," he recalls. But it was Canadian woodturner Leon Lacoursiere who

All photos courtesy the artist unless otherwise indicated

ABOVE

Although he completes the cutting and shaping with the work mounted on the lathe, there's always some hand-detailing to do, especially when finishing. Fein prefers to do this work outdoors, on his deck.

OPPOSITE

Untitled Platter, 2006. Jarrah burl, maple burl; 1¾" deep x 18" diameter. "I love the combination of spirals and wild burls," Fein says. "The movement of the spirals and the wildness of the burl create a perfect foil for each other. In this case, the lightness of the maple burl optically enhances the effect of the spiral."

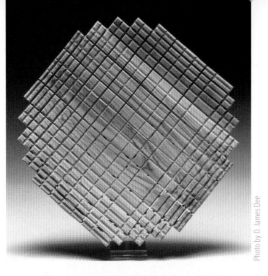

RIGHT

Untitled, 2007. Olive; 1½" high x 15½" wide x 15½" deep. "When I opened up this piece of olive, the linearity of the grain, along with the dark edge, suggested squares. I have done large squares and this was an extension of the idea. Gradation and irregularity."

provided the inspiration for Fein's technical approach. "He showed me a picture of his lathe, which has a built-in drill press, cross feed, and much more," Fein recalls. "The idea of using other tools to do part of the work was revolutionary to me at the time. I found that as I moved away from imitating the many generous teachers and critics I had encountered, I saw the machinist I

All pieces start with determining the shape and then opening up the wood, creating my canvas. The texture, pattern, and inclusions all are considered before I start cutting.

always have been was now making things in wood and that, to my great satisfaction, the pursuit of form and aesthetic value had been added to my lifelong fascination with making things."

Discussing his development as an artist, Fein says, "When I started out, I spent my time perfecting my craft. I then concentrated on form. In hindsight, as I developed my own style, I sort of gave up the craft portion of what I was doing to concentrate on the forms in my head, which is always bursting with ideas. I asked the wood to do things it sometimes refused to do and I had to beat it into shape. Now that I've developed my own approach, I've been getting back to the craft—that is, technical, as well as design, excellence."

ABOVE

4 Points, 2006. Claro walnut, 1¾" high x 17½" wide x 17½" deep. "*Four Points* started out as an experiment in vanishing points. Each set of six lines has a common point some 28 inches off the center, with the piece rotated to produce the pattern and four vanishing points. The diagonal line of light wood in the claro walnut is perfectly sited."

OPPOSITE

Untitled Platter, 2007. Bubinga, coolabah burl; 2½" deep x 19" diameter. "This piece was drawn out to feature a round piece of coolabah burl I had. The thickness and uniformity of the blank was a great foil for the burl."

Inspired by Natural Patterns

BELOW TOP

Fein's home sits on the lake shore adjacent to a state park. Fein's workshop is in the low structure to the left of the main house.

BELOW BOTTOM

Fein's current studio—previously he worked in the basement—looks through the screened porch onto the water, keeping him in touch with the natural patterns that inspire his designs.

During the week, Fein lives and works in New York City where his life is full of activity. On weekends, he and his wife, Fiona, are at home on the edge of a state park in northwestern New Jersey. "As I work at my lathe, I look out of two large windows at the light dancing on lake waters and an occasional parade of native swans floating by," Fein says.

Fein explains why he loves turning: "I'm a turner because the first time I held a gouge to wood, about ten years ago, I felt immediately as if I'd come home to some place I'd never been before. It was one of the most natural, effortless things I'd ever done. I have always seen myself as a maker and after years of working with my brain and a pencil, I felt I was back on track. Woodturning puts me in touch with something essential in my nature that provides a deep satisfaction in my life."

Fein draws his inspiration from the patterns he finds all around him. He finds great inspiration in the natural world: a thin coating of ice on a lake crunched up against a bulkhead, a bloom of forsythia flowers in Central Park, the details on a leaf in a lily pond, the designs found in the bark of lignum vitae, a ravine carved by streams, and patchy moss growing on shale. In the man-made world, Fein draws inspiration from everything, from architecture to patterns created by items on market shelves.

"My work often starts with an idea I've been tossing around in my head for weeks," he explains "Usually, I explore it on paper before choosing a piece of wood. I work out the geometry, and then determine how to set up my jig to accomplish the design. Because I rarely make exactly the same piece more than once, it is a challenge I really enjoy. If the cuts required by the new design are significantly different from those I've done before, I devise new linkages between the spindle and the jig, for example when I went from radial to lateral cuts, or more recently, when I incorporated lines that move in relation to a vanishing point."

www.harveyfein.net

HOW FEIN WORKS:
BIG SHALLOW PLATTERS

From Fein's point of view, wood is the ideal material. As he explains, "Its warmth, the feel, the smell, the dust, the chips, the oil, the wax, sanding, shaping—everything about wood appeals to me." For Fein's complex designs to succeed, the wood must be bone-dry and tight-grained. That is why he tends to work with kiln-dried tropical hardwoods. "I choose a wood with surface features I believe will complement the design and then rough out the shape I need—usually a large, shallow platter about one-inch thick. As the initial process reveals the particular features of the wood I've chosen, I frequently modify my design or even change it altogether. Sometimes I draw parts of the design on the surface of the wood to determine placement, especially if there are prominent surface features that present design or structural challenges. I first cut the face of the platter, then the back."

Fein works on a Stubby 1000 lathe, with its movable bed and auxiliary wing providing the frame for a whole set of modifications. He has cut a passage from the auxiliary bed to the main bed, added an indexing bar to the side of the main bed, and fitted a low-speed drive motor with a foot pedal to control speed of rotation. Fein has extended the spindle, which has indexing stops, so he can get a router behind the workpiece. Unlike many lathe artists, Fein has yet to explore carving, painting, or other off-lathe techniques. "Until they are ready to be finished, my pieces rarely leave the lathe," he says.

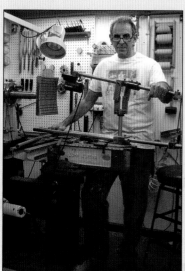

Fein has augmented his Stubby-brand lathe with a variety of jigs, auxiliary tools, and extensions. By using the lathe as a platform, he can precisely control the movement of the cutters on the surface of the workpiece—in this shot, the square of walnut at center left.

Fein reduces the thickness of the workpiece using a powered cutter mounted on auxiliary lathe ways (the two parallel bars below his forearm). To avoid breathing exotic wood dusts, Fein wears a full-head mask with its own supply of filtered outside air.

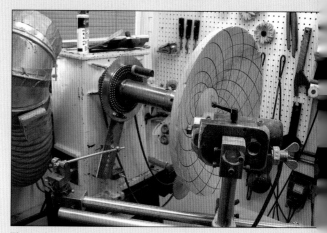

The indexing head mounted on the lathe spindle, left, mates with a traveling arm. The apparatus, combined with the powered cutter mounted on the vertical shaft in the right foreground, allows Fein to cut a controlled series of spirals in the face of the workpiece.

The lathe's spindle extension allows the artist to polish the inside of a large piece without mechanical interference. Fein's specialty is developing technical solutions like this one.

BUTCH SMUTS

Keeping It Simple Is the Best Investment

For most of his working life, Butch Smuts was a wildlife ecologist, later expanding his career into environmental management. He traveled extensively around Southern Africa and other parts of the world. Smuts now resides and works in the South African Lowveld town of Nelspruit, a few hours drive from Kruger National Park. His new home and purpose-built studio are amongst beautiful granite outcrops and indigenous bush on a country estate ten minutes drive from town.

During his life, Smuts maintained a strong interest in woodwork. "I've always loved working with wood and made most of the hardwood furniture in our home," he says. As a boy, he attended the Michaelis School of Art at Worcester, in South Africa's Cape Province. "My teachers introduced me to painting and woodcarving and I hand-carved my first simple bowl out of wood there in 1962," Smuts explains. "As a child,

Apart from the blood, sweat, and tears associated with large dry turnings, you need a good dose of natural dexterity and a modicum of strength.

I made wooden toys and I won my first woodcarving competition as a young Boy Scout. I now find it difficult to measure these early influences, but I will never discount them, as certain memories persist."

Certainly, his love of woodwork endured, because forty years later, he retired early to make a new career

All photos by Wayne Hayward

ABOVE

Smuts turns a Lombardy poplar burl. "When I work on a large project I may spend a day or more preparing the wood for the lathe," Smuts says. "Where nature's agents—that's termites, fungi or the elements—have sculpted a special piece of wood, keeping things together becomes critical. Low lathe speeds, sharp tools and a steady hand are vital."

OPPOSITE TOP

Trilobate, 2006. Resin-tree burl; 10" high x 27½" wide. *Trilobate*, a multi-axis turning, began as a very large burl from an African tree, gathered during Smuts' career as a wildlife ecologist. By multi-axis turning Smuts can hollow the inside of the forms on the lathe, but then it is hand-carving to shape the bottom, texture the wood, and finish it.

OPPOSITE BOTTOM

Trilobate. Detail of carving and texturing on the underside. All shaping of the underside is done by hand.

Intending to hollow the small vessel in the middle of the photo, Smuts bolts the 230-pound block of resin tree burl onto a square piece of 1¼"-thick medium density fiberboard, with an array of steel faceplates (right) to counter-balance the load. He uses a steel frame to retain the blank on the MDF board. A 12"-steel faceplate connects all this apparatus to the lathe spindle.

as a wood artist. "Apart from being stimulating, challenging, and rewarding, I guess that I became a woodturner because woodturning provided new and creative ways to work with wood." In addition, Smuts has been interested in art all of his life, taking the opportunity on his international travels to visit galleries and museums. Not surprisingly, he says, "Other influences include the rich array of ethnic designs that have been developed throughout Africa."

A Wonderful Stock of Wood

Smuts says he has built his woodturning career around his wonderful stock of wood. "My wanderings as an ecologist allowed me to collect timber and many large burls, mainly from dead trees, elephant damage, or those cut down during development projects. If I have a special piece of wood, then I will attempt to bring out the best in it. I have always enjoyed turning big bowls, especially those created using beautiful hardwoods such as leadwood, tamboti, wild olive, pink ivory, mopane, and resin tree. Because of the hard and abrasive nature of many of these woods, I have made my own heavy carbide-tipped tools." The work is just as hard as it sounds. "Technical challenges for a one-man operation include chainsaw preparation of blanks weighing more than 200 pounds, mounting them onto the lathe, and then the dusty, and sometimes

Dune Landscape II, 2005. Resin tree burl; 6½" high x 27½" wide. To hollow a form like this, Smuts centers each vessel on the lathe, using the apparatus shown in the photo above.

dangerous, operation of roughing the work to a more balanced state."

It is clear Smuts is still in love with the turning process. His enormous multi-axis bowls, for example, are a serious challenge he has solved with typical efficiency. "The wonderful thing about woodturning and its technical challenges is it can often be

Many of my designs are influenced by nature, but others are geometric, with the chosen shapes or designs being adapted to fit the rim.

used to develop new artistic features. If, for example, a triple-axis bowl is designed well, then the point where the three bowls intersect creates an interesting three-faceted sculptural feature. Also, hand shaping the underside of each bowl is an opportunity to play with a variety of surface textures."

The Need for Self-Expression

Despite his obvious love of turning, like many other contemporary turners, Smuts finds himself spending less time on the lathe. He explains it well: "We probably all started off having the lathe define almost everything we did. Some well-known artists still earn an honest living doing just that and I also do it from time to time. I let the wood and the lathe do much of the talking, so I can relax and enjoy watching the colors and shape appear. If I have an exceptional piece of wood, I often will turn a simple bowl or platter to display these features—keeping it simple is often the best investment. However, I have a growing need to do more work away from the lathe. The need for self-expression could be related partly to a growing repertoire of skills and ideas, or to the need to produce something new, exciting, personal, and

Out of Africa, 2004. African blackwood, pink ivory, round-leaved kiaat burl inlay; 5½" high x 10⅛" wide. Alongside his large turnings, Smuts also makes delicate little objects such as this vase with a wide rim of thin blackwood and inlays of African motifs.

marketable. The natural feelings of self-expression have to represent an important progression in the career of any artist. Sometimes I spend less than 10 percent of my time doing the turning. To me, lathe art is less about turning techniques and more about discovery and self-expression. Thank goodness, though, for all of those who have helped develop new lathes, tools, and work-holding technology. They have certainly made life easier for all of us."

In contrast to his larger pieces, which he sells predominantly in South Africa, Smuts has developed an international reputation and market for the quality of his delicate inlay bowls. The bowls are masterpieces of design and technical control, tiny works that could not be a greater contrast to his enormous robust pieces. The designs he creates for the smaller pieces are immensely varied and his lifelong observations of design are clearly a great help. "Although many of the designs I choose are influenced by nature or specific human interest themes, others are geometric with the chosen shapes or designs being adapted to fit the available rim area."

The contemporary turned wood movement has become a truly international phenomenon, and as a result, the work on the newly global market often has a sense of place that never existed during the more parochial early days. Butch Smuts produces work that is overwhelmingly the result of his African heritage. First, the woods he uses are not found anywhere else and they evoke strong images of the South African veld. Secondly, the visual themes of many of his pieces reflect Smut's life as an ecologist. If you add his amazing skill in creating both large, robust pieces as well as delicate, finely cut assemblages, you have the work of a unique craftsman.

While Smuts is happy to make both large and small work for now, it seems he is preparing for the future. He asks, "Is it true the size of your work decreases as your age increases? Is this a function of shrinking enthusiasm and physical strength? I've decided to prepare for this eventuality, the point in my career when I may look at a large chunk of leadwood and rather than see a huge bowl hidden inside of it, I will see two or three smaller ones." Whichever he decides to make, we can be sure it will be beautiful.

Nocturnal Surround, 2004. African blackwood, sneezewood, pau marfim inlay; 6½" high x 11⅝ diameter. The intersecting fretsawn teardrop patterns play wonderfully off the circular lathe work.

Avian Menagerie, 2004. African blackwood, pink ivory, round-leaved kiaat burl inlay; 6⅝" high x 12⅛" wide. Smuts finishes his bowls to a fine degree of perfection, "usually down to 800-grit sandpaper and 0000 steel wool. Then I wipe on a few coats of Danish oil before waxing and polishing by hand."

After cutting thin sections of round-leaved kiaat burl on the bandsaw, Smuts tapes them onto a support board in order to sand them smooth.

Smuts uses carbon paper to trace patterns onto the underside of an African blackwood bowl rim.

Using a variable speed scroll saw, Smuts saws the inlay openings out of the blackwood bowl.

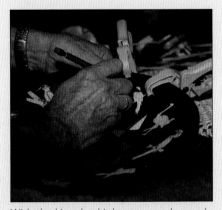

With the kiaat burl inlay veneer clamped in place on the underside of the bowl rim, Smuts transfers the cutout shapes.

He cuts the inlay shapes with the scroll saw, and then fits them into the blackwood rim.

Smuts uses a scalpel and low-viscosity cyanocrylic adhesive to glue the shapes into the bowl rim. He runs the glue into the saw kerfs from both sides.

RON FLEMING

More Ideas Than I Can Ever Produce

Ron Fleming purchased an old incinerator in Tulsa twenty-five years ago and converted it into his home and studio. The updated historical building is on the edge of town and is surrounded by a creek, woods, and flower gardens. "I am practically surrounded by a nature preserve," he says. "It is peaceful here and I have many

---

My work shouldn't look like it came from a lathe or machine and I spend time figuring out how a design can be laid out on the turned form.

---

gardens and sources of inspiration all around me. It is amazing how I can just step outside and see an image for a new piece. My nearest neighbor is more than a block away, so I am never bothered by outside distractions to keep me from my work. I am totally surrounded by nature, which I believe has been one of the biggest influences on me."

Fleming's first career was as a professional illustrator and designer, with agents in New York and San Francisco making it possible for him to remain in his home state of Oklahoma and work out of his home studio. "I've been fortunate to live in my home state," Fleming says. "I could have done better if I had moved to New York or California, but I guess I am a small town person. I like the laid-back lifestyle."

When asking woodturners about others who have influenced them, the leading artists in the field quite

All photos courtesy the artist

ABOVE

With a large workpiece still mounted on the lathe, Fleming creates the bold surface texture using traditional carving tools.

OPPOSITE

African Fern Basket, 2004. Redwood; 14" high x 13" diameter. The wild ferns that grow in the hippo trails of the Okavango Delta of Western Botswana inspired *African Fern Basket*.

Here is the entrance to Fleming's Hearthstone Studios, a converted incinerator on the edge of Tulsa.

From Sketch to Wood

"I keep a sketchbook or camera handy most of the time and will generally do a rough sketch to save for later development," he says. "I seem to have more ideas than I can ever produce. If I am ever not in the creative mood, and I need to produce work for a show, all I have to do is refer to my sketchbook. When I am in the creative mood, I usually design a whole series of pieces and only produce a few of them. My work is very time consuming. From the thought process, to the finished piece, usually takes several weeks or even months. The ideas come rather quickly, as do working out the designs and details involved. It is the technical process of working with wood that takes up the time."

"I like to do work that continually challenges me," Fleming explains. "There is a certain order I must use to create the image I have in mind. It takes both form and design to really make a piece stand out. One will not stand without the other. Woodturning is a natural way for me to combine my capabilities as an artist and a

often offer unexpected names, bringing work far from the field of woodwork into the mix. That is particularly true of Fleming, due to his previous career in illustration. "One artist in particular who

---

When I am in the creative mood, I usually design a whole series of pieces and only produce a few of them. The technical process of working with wood takes up the time.

---

has influenced my work is Aubrey Beardsley. His method of drawing using nature with the human figure in a stylized manner has set his work aside from other artists and intrigued me." Old English, Greek and Roman styles of carving have also influenced Fleming's unique approach. His inspiration is the natural world and most of his ideas come from seeing a particular plant, tree, bird or animal that interests him. He then transforms and stylizes the images, working out the designs in sketchbooks.

Fleming's converted brick studio has large windows that let in ample natural light.

craftsman. Most of the time it is about how I can use the lathe to establish a blank to carve on. You always must have a beautiful form with which to work. When I create my vessels, I look to the lathe only as a basis for my carving. I prefer my work shouldn't look like it came from a lathe or machine and I spend time figuring out how a design can be laid out on the turned form. I am always thinking of composition and balance in this process and can spend several months carving or painting a single piece."

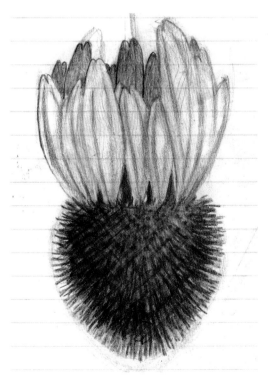

ABOVE

Echinacea, 1992. Dogwood burl and maple; 12½" high x 8½" diameter. Fleming was admiring cone flowers growing in his garden when the idea for this piece came to him.

LEFT TOP & BOTTOM

Fleming keeps a sketchbook and a camera handy so he can record ideas as they develop and save them for later development.

The Guardian, 2005. Walnut with copper patina; 38½" high x 14" diameter. The head of the mythological griffin and the body texture of the African crocodile inspired Fleming to create a very large piece.

Childhood in the Indiana Countryside

Fleming was something of a prodigy in the arts and as a child, received a great deal of support and encouragement from his family and teachers. He began studying illustration and painting at eight years of age and completed his first commercial work at thirteen. "I did get an early start in my career. I always knew art was what I wanted do to do with my life. For many years, I watched and helped my father and grandfather work in wood. I have fond memories of working in my grandfather's shop and he always encouraged my desire to become an artist and understand creative and technical processes."

The influence of the natural world came early as well, as Fleming was raised in the country and spent a great deal of time hiking and camping as a child.

"I loved nature and always was interested in the many facets of it. I was always observing and learning, thinking, and searching for a way to express the thoughts and feelings I had about nature."

While Fleming often works with exotic timbers, such as pink ivory, cocobolo, and African blackwood, he also uses discarded woods as often as possible. "There are a lot of walnut, pecan, hackberry, sycamore and oak trees in this area. When I hear a tree species I like to turn is coming down, I try to make arrangements to get as much of it as I can. The beauty and potential of wood has always intrigued me. It is fairly easily manipulated and its pattern and grain are always unique and different."

www.hearthstonestudios.com

In poetic words, Fleming convincingly conveys the passion he feels for the nature that inspires him: "Whether it be the falling leaves of autumn swirling into a frozen form, or a single flower bud unfolding in spring, each piece gives me an opportunity to make a statement about the never-ending rituals of nature's evolution. Each form in wood becomes a captured moment of its own existence and every vessel gives me a way to express my feelings about the things I see around me and to share these visions with others."

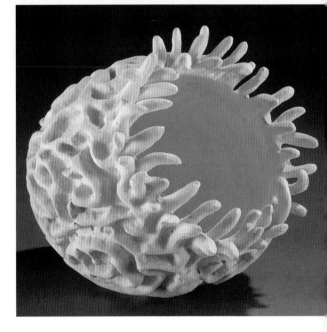

ABOVE TOP

New Beginnings, 2003. Redwood burl; 11" high x 18" diameter. Like *African Fern Basket*, *New Beginnings* is derived from the wild ferns of Botswana.

ABOVE BOTTOM

Spongula, 2001. Bleached madrone; 11½" high x 11" diameter. The giant vase sponge inspired *Spongula*. Fleming used madrone (arbutus) burl, which warps and twists, to create the misshapen form.

LEFT

Athena, 2004. Pink ivory; 10" high x 7" diameter. *Athena* was inspired by the leaves of the *Phalaenopsis mania* orchid.

PETER HROMEK

You Find These Shapes Everywhere in Nature

Anyone who has worked on the lathe will be fascinated by Peter Hromek's multi-axis pieces, because they seem to defy logic. You can't see how he could have hollowed them out, nor what the lathe had to do with it. Many people find Hromek's pieces so startling they can't quite believe they are made of wood.

Arriving at the designs was not an immediate process, Hromek explains. "At the start I used to make spindle-like bodies which were laid on their side, but then I had the idea of putting some of the forms together to make them stand up. I turned three shapes exactly the same, then fitted them together," Hromek said. "It wasn't so easy because the walls were only about a quarter-inch thick and, as everybody knows, wood moves. That was how my first 'Tripod' was created and then it took me almost five years to work out how to repeat it."

Hromek continues, "I wanted to hollow the complete form and I realized that would be possible only if I hollowed it through narrow openings in the tips.

When I feel my work somehow touches the viewers, then I think my job is well done.

The results deceive the viewer because although there is a big opening in the vessel, it is not hollowed out through that opening. It's exciting to let the hollowing of three shapes in one piece of wood penetrate each other and it's hardly possible to imagine it was created on a lathe. It's wonderful to bring together shapes,

All photos courtesy the artist

ABOVE

Hromek displays the mystifying interior of a three-lobed vessel. "It's exciting to let the hollowing of three shapes in one piece of wood penetrate each other," he says.

OPPOSITE

Venus #1, 2006. Box alder, partly stained; 16" high. This multi-axis turning, made from one large piece of wood, *Venus #1* exemplifies Hromek's current work. Deceptively, the three lobes were each hollowed out from what has become their bottom ends. The opening at the top was partially formed on the lathe, and partially carved.

which by themselves are quite ordinary, and create something completely different and unusual." This improbability is what makes Hromek's work unique. He has built on a sound sense of form and line, which made his simple hollow forms work so well, and he has taken it to an entirely different level of sophistication. His vessels look complex enough, but only by observing just how difficult the process is can we appreciate Hromek's expertise.

A Multi-Faceted Career

Hromek grew up in the Czech Republic and qualified as a precision mechanic. In 1969, he moved to Germany and studied technical engineering. During all this time he says he had a love of craft work and art. "I used to make jewelry, just for fun," he says. A creative spirit, he also was playing bass in a bluegrass band and soon started to make guitars. "I read all of the books about stringed instruments I could get. Although my guitars were made to a professional standard, it was hard to sell many because I lacked marketing experience. So I wrote a book about building guitars, then gave up."

Hromek then worked for six years as a model maker in chemical plants, but computers eventually took over the job. Forced to contemplate another change in career, he decided to try his hand as a craftsman again. "I bought a small table-top lathe and started to turn. I did not know anything about it and I was just scraping everything. Again, I went to a library, this time to read all of the books I could get about turning. Of course, reading and turning are two different things."

ABOVE TOP

Spindle, 2006. Ebonized robinia; 13" long. There is a serenity about *Spindle*. It is simply a conventional vessel cleverly cut to show grain in unexpected ways and then laid down in repose.

ABOVE BOTTOM

Submarine, 2005. Sugar maple burl; 15" long. Perhaps the simplest of Hromek's logic-beaters, it should not be possible to turn a piece like *Submarine* on the lathe. To imagine how it was done, it is necessary to see it partly as a spindle turning, partly as a vessel, and partly as a carving.

OPPOSITE

Paradise, 2007. Maple; 13" high. Says Hromek, "I have heard people say my work is sensual. I like that idea."

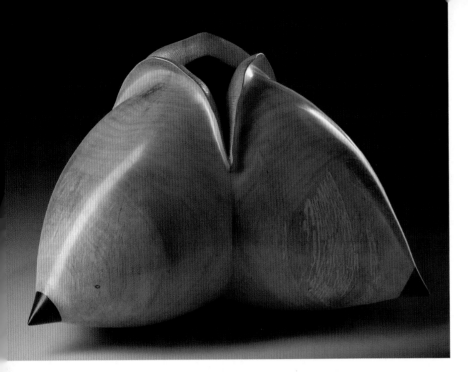

Venus #2, 2004. Alder, 16" diameter. Venus #2 emphasizes the sensual curves that so please the maker.

Despite the difficult beginnings, Hromek was sure he had found his profession. "Right from the start I was so fascinated by this kind of work that I couldn't stop, but I didn't realize how hard it would be. I used to cook at nights in a local restaurant and turn in the daytime. I found a translation

---

They look very organic to me, like seeds, seed pods, leaves, flowers, fruit, parts of the human body.

---

of Richard Raffan's book on woodturning design (page xii) and this became my Bible. I used to turn many natural-edged bowls, vases, and so on, which I still like to do."

Hromek now has the lifestyle he always wanted. "I reside in a small village in the middle of Germany with my wife, a dog, and three cats. My wife is also an artist and she makes her art out of paper, another wood product. We have a big garden with many fruit trees and flowers, and we grow some vegetables. In German, people call us 'land eggs.' We have good neighbors. One

of them makes figurative works in ceramics and concrete, and once or twice a year, we organize exhibitions in our houses and gardens and invite other artists to exhibit with us. The visitors come mostly from the cities."

Finding His Own Style

Hromek has gone far beyond his early simple fascination with wood and basic turning. "Today when I design my sculptured vessels I don't necessarily care much about the grain. The wood has become a carrier of form, although it still influences the finished piece." He must have succeeded in surpassing people's expectations, as he explains: "Often at exhibitions people ask me if my pieces are made of wood. They ask me that even when they are standing right in front of the object. I found it hard to understand, but then I realized they are not able to relate the forms to wood."

When you are hollowing on more than one axis, the process takes careful planning. Hromek says he carries ideas for a new design around in his head for days or even weeks. "When I start a multi-axis object, I first make a technical drawing at a scale of 1:1. That helps me to define the shape and how to chuck the piece, what part I am able to turn, and what I have to mill or carve by hand." The process is far from the simple turning that first attracted Hromek, but he believes it is still relatively simple, as he explains: "It's like many other woodturners who are moving away from turning to free-forming, but the turning is still a very important part of my work and I don't use any special tools or chucking methods. All of my works are hollowed out on the lathe, but outside there is not so much turning."

Now he believes he has found his own style in this work. "They look very organic to me, like cells. You find the shapes everywhere in nature—seeds, seed pods, leaves, flowers, fruit, and parts of the human body. When I feel my work somehow touches the viewers, then I think my job is well done. I have heard people say my work is sensual. I like that idea."

ABOVE LEFT

Small heaven #1, 2005. Sugar maple burl; 15" wide. *Small heaven #1*, turned on three axes, leaves the viewer wondering how it could have been hollowed on a lathe. Hromek did much of the hollowing through the openings at the ends of the lobes, not through the vessel's mouth.

ABOVE RIGHT

Tripod, 2002. Maple; 14" high. An early piece, *Tripod* was turned as three discrete forms, which were then cut at the rim and glued together. The work required endless trial-fitting and adjusting, and Hromek wanted to achieve the same effect in a single piece of wood.

LEFT

Small Heaven #2, 2003. Stained cherry; 16" wide. Hromek has plugged the openings in the ends of the lobes, leaving no trace of how the form was hollowed out. The ebonized exterior contrasts wonderfully with the rich wood texture of the interior.

Hromek has prepared the maple blank for a multi-axis turning. At this stage, the solid log weighs around 55 pounds. The final vessel will weigh about 2 pounds.

Starting from a cylinder, Hromek has cut a spigot for the chuck (left) and turned the basic bell shape. Now he opens out what will become the top opening of the vessel.

Hromek remounts the blank between centers, on pre-determined diagonal points. He balances it by screwing lead weights onto the wood.

Hromek turns the first of three more spigots. Each spigot will subsequently be mounted in the lathe chuck so an opening can be turned.

Hromek remounts the blank three times to turn three equally spaced spigots. The lead weights have to be moved each time.

With the blank remounted in the chuck on one of the new spigots, Hromek bores the deep hole that begins a new opening. The hole penetrates the center opening he hollowed at the start.

Hromek hollows out the new section with a gouge. You can see in the whirling wood a shadow view of the final shape of this part of the vessel.

The artist repeats the process twice more and the three-lobed shape begins to emerge. When all of the insides have been hollowed, he turns the outside of each with support from the lathe's tailstock (right).

Hormek continues to shape the wood using a power carving tool mounted on the lathe's tool post, at right, while he slowly rotates the workpiece by hand. He's left lots of wood opposite the lobes for later shaping to form the lips around the vessel's finished opening.

With the piece remounted on its central spigot, Hromek turns the final shape of the base. After refining the details by carving, Hromek sets the piece aside so the wood can dry out, after which he will complete the carving. The walls are about ¼" thick.

WILLIAM MOORE

The Contrasting Relationships of Wood and Metal

While the majority of woodturners are self-taught, the art-school educated William Moore is a notable exception. Today, he divides his time between teaching art and creating sculptural vessels that combine metal spinning and woodturning.

Moore lives and works in western Oregon, about 16 miles west of Portland in an area called Helvetia. Not exactly a town, Helvetia is a wide spot in the road with a handful of houses and a tavern surrounded by family farms. Descendants of the original Swiss settlers own many of the farms. Moore and his family reside in what was once the community dance hall across the street

The hollow wood vessels are much too fragile to withstand the forces of the metal spinning process. So I turn a solid duplicate from hard maple, onto which I actually spin the metal.

from the tavern. Next door to their home is Moore's 1,400 square foot shop, filled with equipment and featuring four lathes, including a Oneway and a Yates American #13 patternmaker's lathe.

The influence of woodturning came early in William Moore's life. Rather than coming from his father's garage workshop, as is frequently the case, it came from his mother, who acquired a lathe in the early 1950s. "She loved Bob Stockdale's work and I learned to appreciate his work through her," says Moore. "She taught me to turn on her 1950s Craftsman lathe."

Photo by David James Clark

ABOVE

The works of Moore require meticulous planning, measuring, and fitting.

OPPOSITE

Inverness, 2000. Oak burl, bronze; 10" high x 10" wide x 5" deep. "The metal portions are not decorative additions, but rather are integral to the whole," Moore says. "The body is turned oak burl. Mimicking traditionally styled handles of kitchen cutlery, the wood on either side of the handle's bronze spine are of the same oak. All other elements are bronze. To provide contrast, some bronze elements have a brushed finish. Others have a speckled texture with a brown patina."

Euphrates, 1990. Madrone, copper; 64" high x 17½" wide x 11½" deep. "I created *Euphrates* when I was interested in ceremony, ritual, and symbolic objects," Moore says. "The stand, the vessel, and its stopper create a totem-like composition."

Equilibrium, 2006. Maple burl, copper, bronze; 11⅜" high x 23½" wide x 13¼" deep. Recently, Moore has turned toward exploring gesture and balance to create a sense of movement. In *Equilibrium*, he combines multiple-axis hollow forms with spun metal to create a sense of equilibrium, or coming to rest.

The term "sculpture" is often applied to works in the field of contemporary turned wood art, yet very few artists are actually trained sculptors. William Moore is an

The fitting of metal to wood can be slow and labor-intensive. The forms combine well because they were all created on the lathe."

exception. As a student studying sculpture, he was initially inspired by Henry Moore and later by Philip Grausman. He went on to be influenced by an array of sculptural approaches, as well as the important design movements of the late-nineteenth and twentieth centuries, including Art Nouveau, the Arts & Crafts movement, and the Bauhaus.

Discovering the Lathe's Potential

During his studies in art school, Moore explored a range of materials and created sculptures in raised copper, plaster, clay, welded steel, carved stone, cast bronze, plastic, fiberglass, and wood. While he found all of the materials interesting, only wood had properties that suited him.

"Wood had some resistance, unlike clay, but could be manipulated more easily than steel," Moore says. "Stone weighed a ton and was too resistant to change. Wood has rich variety of color and texture and its form can be altered with a variety of tools, most of which I enjoy working with."

In the late 1970s, Moore's mother gave him her lathe. At the time, he was constructing wood sculpture. Initially, he did not know how he would use the lathe, imagining he would just turn gifts for friends. He rediscovered the lathe's potential as a tool once it was in his shop and began making forms for the constructed wood sculptures he was building. Soon he was exploring forms he could create better with a lathe than with any other tool in his shop. Encountering Steven Hogbin's split-turned objects in *Fine Woodworking* magazine (page x) showed him even greater potential for the lathe. "I was dazzled," Moore says. "Thinking of turnings as objects that could be altered after they came off the lathe was a revelation." Seeing Lynn Hull's spun metal works influenced Moore to think about combining turned wood and spun metal. Moore came to create strong relationships between the wood and metal elements in his work.

How Moore Works: Wood and Metal

William Moore's process often begins with drawn ideas he further refines in the turning process. Next, he creates turned wood elements, followed by developing the spun and/or fabricated metal elements to complement the wood and make the composition whole. He must complete the two processes separately and once he has created the metal elements, the wood may need to be carved and tweaked to achieve the perfect fit.

Photo by David James Clark

To spin metal, Moore presses a flat disk of copper or brass onto a hard maple form.

"The hollow wood vessel forms in my work are much too fragile to withstand the forces of the metal spinning process," Moore explains. "Once the wood elements of a piece are finished, I create a template of the turned form and then turn a solid duplicate pattern from hard maple, which is the form onto which I actually spin the metal."

Moore believes the lathe strongly defines his sculptures. "I am drawn to the character

of the symmetrical forms I create on the lathe," he says. "They have a crisp, sharp clarity from any perspective. Most of my compositions are about the contrasting relationships of wood and metal. The forms combine well because they were all created on the lathe." The lathe ultimately represents "just a quarter to a third of the time to realize the final piece," Moore says. "The fitting of metal to wood can be slow and labor-intensive. On some pieces, it may require carving to form portions of the piece."

In many of Moore's pieces, the metal parts are not a single spun form but rather several made separately and silver-soldered together. The careful fitting together of parts before soldering and the finishing of all of the soldered seams afterward is a slow and laborious process. Patination of the metal is the final step before he assembles the work.

Having solved the aesthetic and technical aspects, a work holds little interest for Moore unless it suggests new possibilities. "I most enjoy exploring a new idea, and solving the compositional and technical problems," Moore says. "Every step of the process in creating a piece is a challenge."

Works in progress, sketches of designs, and tools fill the studio. "I am not known for neatness," says Moore, who recalls seeing a photo of Alexander Calder in his studio, where hand tools and materials covered every square inch of space. "It made me feel at home," Moore says. "I clean up occasionally. After all, you need to clear a surface to work on sometimes."

VAUGHN RICHMOND

Technical Challenges Are the Most Exciting

Many contemporary woodturners struggle to describe the relationship between their turning and the additional work they do on their pieces. Not so Vaughn Richmond, who simply, but elegantly, says: "Some of my woodturning may have an element of sculpture, and some of my sculptures may have an element of

---

My work is divided between what I know I can do technically and what I would like to be able to do.

---

woodturning." The statement wonderfully sums up much of what has happened to woodturning during the last twenty years.

"My work is divided between what I know I can do technically and what I would like to be able to do," Richmond continues. "I regard the technical challenges as the most exciting ones. I enjoy developing the knowledge and techniques to deal with a new design idea. The process can be slow. An idea or an influence planted in the library of the mind may take many years to develop. The result may be really pleasing, or fizzle out and be sent back to storage for the future. I rarely sketch my ideas and am fortunate I can visualize a finished piece and the steps needed to make it. This also gives me the flexibility to change the design while I am making the piece. Often I venture onto another path as inspiration takes over from common sense. The shelves of half-completed work testify to this."

Photo by Dean Malcolm. Other photos by Victor France unless otherwise indicated.

ABOVE

Richmond perches on a huge boulder among the bush he loves in West Cape Howell National Park, the southernmost point of Western Australia: "A little piece of my world."

OPPOSITE

Fluted Vase, 2006. Sandalwood, gold leaf, pearl shell, acrylic paints; 5½" high x 2¾" diameter. It requires extreme control to create such fine detail on such a small scale. Richmond creates the fluting on a dedicated system using a swing-arm mounted router. The unfluted section actually emphasizes the fluted areas.

As a proud West Australian, Richmond's work is distinguished by a strong sense of place. He works exclusively in timbers that are unique to his region, including jarrah and West Australian she-oak. When viewing his work, the beautiful hand-worked finishes offer a strong first impression. Richmond lovingly polishes his pieces to perfection, bringing out the rich tones of the woods he uses. Next, it is impossible to ignore the meticulous craftsmanship. The quality of Richmond's work is second to none and his superb craftsman exemplifies the importance of painstaking attention to detail.

Many Strong Influences

It is interesting to see how many strong influences there have been on the West Australian artist. "Art Nouveau has impressed me. It seems it was a period of enthusiasm when craftspeople and artists broke away from the mundane. I love its asymmetrical designs and the sensual curves and lines." He also credits fellow West Australian woodworker Greg Collins as being a powerful influence. "In the early

1980s, I had just started to turn and I saw an exhibition of Greg's work. I was impressed by the quality of his finishes and I thought, 'If this is what needs to be done, then I'd better get some more practice in.'" Richmond also credits potter Dame Lucie

I'm comfortable with 'woodturner' as this is my chosen craft.

Rie, who was born in 1902 in Vienna, as a strong inspiration. "I am fascinated by the patterning and decoration techniques on her finely thrown and well proportioned bowls." Woodworker David Pye also deeply affected Richmond. "In the book *David Pye, Woodturner and Carver*, I found phrases that stay with me including 'the workmanship of risk,' 'small differences in the quality of all things matter,' and 'periods of complete absorption and commitment.'"

Richmond puts those ideals into practice and does work in "periods of complete absorption and commitment" for up to a month at a time. When he is done, he shuts his workshop for a couple of weeks and rests. He says it is the best way for him to maintain an interest in the work. Richmond also believes he is fortunate to be able to "take time off by travelling around demonstrating woodturning."

Young people are rarely able to study woodturning at school, but Richmond was fortunate to experience the craft at an early age. Apart from the fact his father was a woodwork teacher for thirty-five years, he also generously acknowledges the guidance of his schoolteachers. "I turned my first piece of wood at high school as part of a

Lightning 1, 2006. Jarrah, acrylic paints; 4" diameter x 2½" high. As with much of Richmond's work, the contrasts emphasize the tones of the wood. The deep, rich tone of the jarrah would not be so obvious by itself, but contrasting it with flat black enhances both the color and figure.

The Warmth of the Wood

As with most people, wood itself is special to Richmond. "Wood is tactile and warm. I'm constantly amazed how nature can produce such endless varieties of color, grain, and texture. I'm fortunate to reside in an area that has some of the world's most beautiful timbers and I have legal access to fallen logs. Collecting the wood is a special part of my woodturning. To walk in the forest, admire the beauty of nature, and know I have the potential to reveal the hidden beauty inside a gnarly old log is something special."

There is not much pretentiousness about Richmond's description of himself. "I'm comfortable with 'woodturner,' as it is my chosen craft. I still find the lathe a fascinating instrument and I have no doubt I still have a lot to learn about lathes and the turning process. The lathe is the most important piece of equipment in my workshop and my work

manual arts subject, along with metalwork and technical drawing. It was a hands-on experience and I'm grateful for the patience of the instructors who showed me how to turn a lumpy old bit of wood into a nice rolling pin." That early experience re-emerged in the early 1980s when Richmond started turning again in response to the demand for quality craft work in wood.

ABOVE

Swisshh, 2005. Sheoak; 15" diameter x 3" high. The dynamic *Swisshh* is typical of the earlier designs that established Richmond's reputation as a superb craftsman.

LEFT

Square, 2006. Sheoak; 6" diameter x 2⅜" high. Richmond plays with the idea of the traditional bowl, capping the bowl form with a raised square pattern that is the exact opposite of what we would expect.

ABOVE

Landscape, 2003. Jarrah burl, Queensland mountain ash inserts; 13⅜" diameter x 2¾" deep. As with *Meeting Place No1*, *Landscape* reflects the scarified Australian landscape. The dots represent the nomadic wanderings of the Aborigines across the land.

RIGHT

Meeting Place No1, 2006. Jarrah burl, pewter, acrylic paints; 11¾" diameter x 1⅜" high. In Aboriginal lore, the winding trail of the Dreamtime serpent links sacred sites. *Meeting Place No1* echoes the stories.

is completed within the limits of the turning process. I have four lathes and they are set up to perform slightly different turning tasks—turning, fluting, hollowing, etc."

Despite acknowledging the lathe as top-dog in the workshop, Richmond's work falls into the familiar modern pattern of on- and off-lathe time. "Some pieces can take several days on the lathe, then several weeks on the bench. I usually have a whole lot of projects happening at the same time and when I have had enough of sanding, I can do some more

---

Some of my woodturning may have an element of sculpture, and some of my sculptures may have an element of woodturning.

---

turning. Sometimes I may have five pieces going, all with different design challenges. Then, there is what I call 'play time'—a few days just trying out new turning or mechanical processes. It is a real buzz when a new idea actually works."

Richmond is a happy, gregarious person, much loved by audiences when he demonstrates. He is likely to say to visitors, "Let's go out in the bush. I can show you some really good trees!" It is fun to talk to him, because he enjoys life so much. "And why wouldn't I?" he would add. "I live in the beautiful state of Western Australia with an easy-going lifestyle, fresh air, glorious beaches, nice wine, and access to some of the world's most beautiful timbers. I work in a great studio at the rear of my house next to a park with tall trees and abundant bird life, and I have a great bunch of woodturning friends." Who can argue with that?

Photo courtesy the artist

ABOVE TOP

Fluted Dish, 2006. Jarrah, pewter, acrylic paints, black coral; 5½" diameter x 1⅝" deep. Fluted platters like this are another of Richmond's signature styles, simple and supremely elegant.

ABOVE BOTTOM

Dark Sun, 2006. Jarrah, pewter, acrylic paints; 13¼" diameter x 1¾" deep. A hymn of praise to the beauty of the wood, *Dark Sun* highlights its sweep of tones from the dark and richly figured heartwood to the lighter, less mottled sapwood.

ROLLY MUNRO

The Lathe Creates Armatures for Major Sculptural Work

Rolly Munro is extraordinary. Of all of the people working in the field of wood art, Munro perhaps deserves the title "artist" more than any other. Although he uses the lathe extensively, it is possible he also brings

---

Art forms are a melding of technique, the physical act of making a piece, and expressing the content within a work.

---

a wider repertoire of skills to his work than other wood artists. His work begins with meticulously made drawings and proceeds through a process defined at all stages by a complete understanding of what the end result will be. His wonderfully textured and enhanced vessels are not only the result of inspired vision, but of considered elements, balanced and complementary.

For example, in *PuhaPuha Form*, he has wonderfully combined the whole sculptural process with surface treatments in a unique combination. Most contemporary turners would have been satisfied with the surface texture, but Munro also has transformed the opening in the top of the vessel so it goes beyond the simple hollow form and becomes a creative tour de force.

Becoming An Artist in New Zealand

Like many other artists, a family member initially influenced Munro, as he explains: "My uncle, John Munro, was an art teacher and a sculptor. That might have influenced me to study art. In my early days as a

All photos courtesy the artist

ABOVE

The dogs frolic with Munro on the beach near their home. Munro draws imagery from the ever-present sea.

OPPOSITE

The Crow of a Small Amphibious Teapot, 2000. Tawa, English walnut, raspberry jam wood, pink ivory wood; 11¾" high x 7¾" diameter. The idea of the piece itself is astonishing enough, but the detail is even more fascinating. Examining the beautifully carved legs more carefully, it is clear the birdlike feet are partly embedded in the ground, possibly an observation by Munro as his feet scuffed the sand on his daily beach walks.

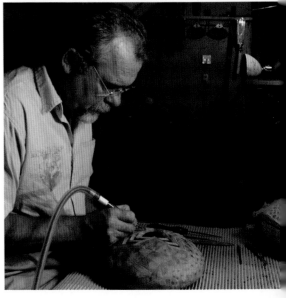

ABOVE

PuhaPuha Form, 1999. Ebonized kauri turned and carved; 7¾" high x 11" diameter. The eloquent surface decoration draws on traditional Maori carving. The intense patterns are both incised and pierced. The complex mouth of the vessel, with its intricate carving, is pure Rolly Munro.

RIGHT TOP

Munro's home in Lower Hutt looks over the city of Wellington, New Zealand.

RIGHT BOTTOM

Munro will spend weeks on a piece to achieve what he wants. "It's a slow journey and it's difficult to justify the time spent other than by saying it's for the love of it."

student of fine arts, I was hugely moved by Jacob Epstein, Henry Moore, Barbara Hepworth, and many other artists, although Moore and Hepworth were the ones who actually used wood." Munro also acknowledges the influence of indigenous Oceanic and New Zealand Maori art forms. "They used wood extensively, but they mixed it with other unexpected media and treatments. Their work was both utilitarian and non-utilitarian," Munro said.

Another powerful influence on Munro's art is the place in which he resides. His home and workshop are near the city of Wellington on New Zealand's North Island. He is near many beaches, has magnificent views of the mountains, and his home is surrounded by hills covered in native trees. It is an evocative environment and his distinctive work echoes it in every way.

The Lathe as a Sculptural Tool

Munro discovered the lathe as a sculptural tool when he was at art school during the 1970s. He had to make components for a design project and says he "began seeing possibilities for the turned form. Later, when I was browsing through a book, I saw a few samples of Bob Stocksdale's natural-edged bowls and I thought I might be able to make a little money to help me though art school by turning wooden bowls." Munro's love of turning remains strong: "Since my first experience on a lathe at age 19, I have loved the pure sensual pleasure of peeling wood. I am now 52 and still experience the same gratification from the sound, the feel, and the aromas as the peelings fly."

Perhaps because he fell into woodturning by default, something he has in common with many other contemporary turners, Munro was not taught how to turn wood or what the various tools do. "I absorbed the process by osmosis, so you can imagine there were many accidents, both good and bad. Much of my early turning equipment was home-built and I'm still interested in tooling." Creating tools has accounted for much of his working time in recent years, as Munro has developed his own line of hollowing tools, somewhat reducing his output of wood art.

There is no "searching for the piece within the wood" for Munro. He always knows exactly what he is going to do before he starts cutting, as he explains: "Art forms are a melding of technique, the physical act of making a piece, and expressing the content within a work. My aim is to seamlessly blend the elements and not to

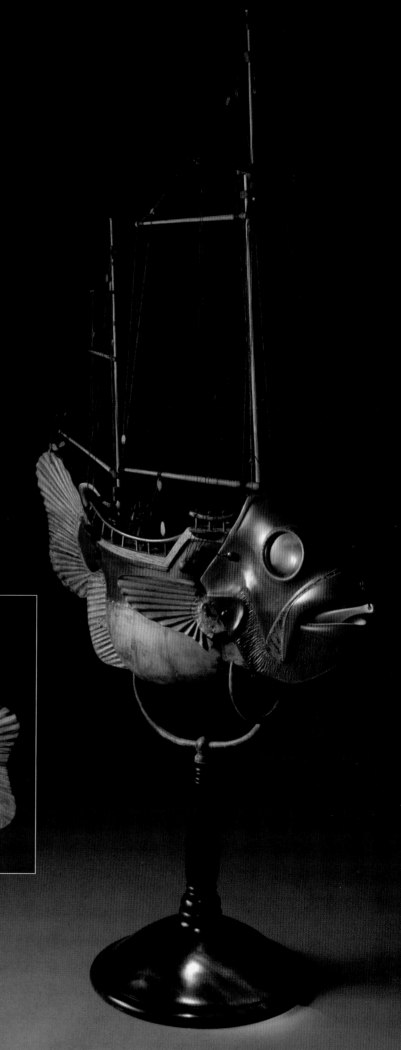

Refit in Lilliput, 1998. Matai, English oak, western red cedar; ebonized pohutukawa and other woods, glass, copper, cotton; carved, turned, assembled, pigmented, patinated and polished; 16½" long x 39½" high x 11¾" wide. Says Munro, "It's an exciting voyage which I hope arrives at unique destinations."

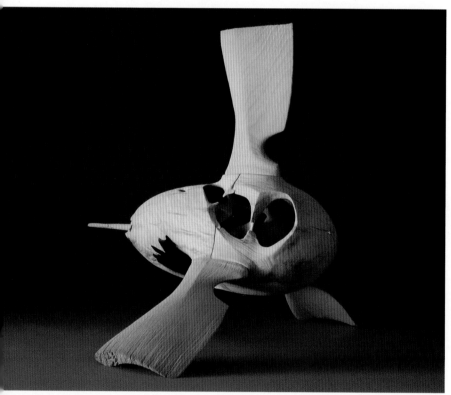

be overpowered by the joy of just boring into a piece of wood. I have a theme before I start. I've worked with marine forms almost exclusively. I make sketches and find samples. Sometimes patterns help me gel my ideas and production methods. The work

Every wood is different. The weight, the color, the smell, the pore structure, the grain directions, and its workability, are like the delectable elements of wine or food. I need to cut it.

may change because of the uncertain nature of wood or because of artistic oversight, but usually my process irons out problems before work on the wood starts."

Looking at a piece such as *Refit in Lilliput*, the range of techniques and materials Munro uses is amazing. He says, "In recent years, I've combined turning, carving and a variety of surface treatments. It's an exciting voyage, which I hope arrives at unique destinations. While I work, I explore and often take time out to make specialized tooling. All the while, I try to keep the original concepts in sight. Occasionally, I stumble upon unseen ideas, and these are sometimes immediately used and sometimes not. It's a slow journey and it's difficult to justify the time spent other than by saying it's for the love of it."

ABOVE TOP

Mahanga Form, 1999. English walnut; 4¼" high x 11" diameter. Says Munro, "It continues the shellfish theme. The palm spikes express clutching tentacles, while the incised design evokes the creature's camouflage of light and water."

ABOVE BOTTOM

Pattern #12 906 431, 2001. New Zealand kauri; turned, carved and sandblasted; 23½" long x 17½" high x 21½" wide. Marine-inspired *Pattern #12 906 431* resembles whale vertebrae washed up on the beach, or some corroded mechanical part, such as a propeller.

www.rollymunro.co.nz

Exploring the Wood

Despite his careful design process, Munro can still enjoy exploring the wood for the sake of it. "Often a turner throws a piece of wood on the lathe just to see what's inside. I don't know of many other materials where that is common. I still do that. Every wood has a different character. The weight, the color, the smell, the pore structure, the grain directions, and its workability are like the delectable elements of wine or food. For me it's an interactive experience. I need to cut it."

For an artist who uses so many different techniques, it is perhaps surprising to hear Munro speak of the lathe with so much passion. It's a carefully reasoned and compelling point of view. "A wood lathe creates a distinctive three-dimensional object eased away from an engineered form by the character of the wood spun on it. It's difficult to conceal the powerful and dominant lines of symmetry in a turned object. Wood is also notoriously unstable, given to distorting, cracking, or rotting in the process of converting it from tree to finished object. Minimizing the wall thickness of an object before drying reduces problems. I discovered woodturning is a very fast wood removal system allowing a blank canvas to be created quite quickly. For me, the forms create armatures for major sculptural work. A typical piece requires a day's turning, but two to three weeks of other processes."

Munro should be better known than he is, but he is not an aggressive self-promoter. His contributions to design in wood art should be better acknowledged. Until then, well-informed students of the craft can continue to enjoy the well-measured output of a remarkable artist.

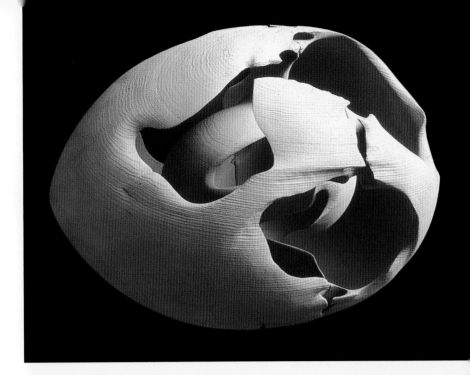

ABOVE TOP

Flotsam, 1990. Kauri wood, turned, carved and sandblasted; 15" wide x 11¾" diameter. Munro was stretching the boundaries of the turning field while most were still making salad bowls. *Flotsam* is a typical example of his early vision. A small tongue and groove lock the two hollowed halves together. The sandblasted shapes evoke wind- and sea-scoured shells found on the beach.

ABOVE BOTTOM

Hollow Form, 1998. Silky oak; 11¾" high x 17½" diameter. One of Munro's simpler pieces, *Hollow Form* still shows his trademark carving. Much of the patterning is indexed and defined on the lathe, then later refined by careful hand carving.

HANS WEISSFLOG

Totally Focused While Turning

When Hans Weissflog's work appeared on the international woodturning scene in the early 1990s, it was unlike anything anyone else was creating. Collectors and artists alike marveled at the intricate design of his works and the technical virtuosity involved in creating them. His small, intricate boxes were linked to

---

A great many of them break in the process. It's a pity nobody collects only my broken pieces, as it would result in large and interesting collections.

---

traditions and approaches that had little in common with the bowls and vessels that dominated the field. The difference in Weissflog's work probably relates to a background considerably different from that of most other artists in the field.

Weissflog began with a three-year apprenticeship in mechanical engineering, eventually becoming a mechanical engineering technician. With a growing interest in design, he then attended Fachhochschule Hildesheim/Holzminden for more than three years. His professor was both a well-known woodturner and the person responsible for woodturning apprenticeships in Germany. "That made it easy for me to become a woodturner," Weissflog says.

Starting with a range of utilitarian objects, such as baby rattles and children's toys, Weissflog learned to design and create larger works, such as lamps and furniture. During those years, he discovered small-lidded

All photos courtesy the artist

ABOVE

Using a skew chisel laid flat, Weissflog rounds over the lattice work.

OPPOSITE

Rocking Bowl, 1996. Cocobolo; 5" high x 6⅝" wide x 5" deep. "With *Rocking Bowl*, I wanted to design a piece with a heavy, massive part that belongs to the earth and a light, pierced-through part to represent heaven," Weissflog says.

boxes provided him with the greatest design opportunities. "With boxes I could create more forms and it was an area not as many people were exploring. I could change the orientation and use smaller pieces of wood, which made more species available to me."

When Weissflog began his career as a woodturner, he intentionally avoided reading books or magazines so he could discover his own style. One day, while visiting a museum, he encountered intricate pierced forms created a century ago by a German turner named Saueracre on an ornamental turning lathe. "The design was dated and the pieces were flat, like a disc," Hans remembers. "But I thought it would be interesting to develop that kind of work with contemporary designs in three dimensions and without using an ornamental lathe. That's how my work started."

Having become known for his small boxes, Weissflog began to explore the potential of the bowl. "Bowl forms presented a challenge and the opportunity to work in different sizes. I wanted to work with native woods such as cherry that weren't dense enough to work well on a smaller scale. Also, larger forms brought more attention to what I was doing, as smaller pieces are often lost in exhibition spaces." He also found it opened up new markets for his work, because some collectors were not interested in the small-scale pieces, but related well to the larger bowl forms that had established the field of artistic woodturning.

RIGHT TOP

The museum gives medieval character to the town of Hildesheim where Weissflog lives.

RIGHT BOTTOM

Weissflog pierces the lattice in a lidded box.

A Medieval German Town

Weissflog resides and works in Hildesheim, Germany. The city, known for its medieval character, sports a rose tree believed to have been planted when the cathedral was first built in the ninth century. There is also the historic marketplace, and the Romanesque St. Michael's Church. Weissflog has reached out to international art galleries to market his work, but collectors often travel to Hildesheim to search him out, largely due to the way he has established himself in the craft/art market.

As Weissflog's collector base grew in the United States, he continued to develop the

market for his work in Europe. Exhibiting at a biannual fair in Frankfurt and an annual exhibition for craft/arts at the Museum fur Kunst und Gewerbe in Hamburg, Weissflog has cultivated collectors. One German fan has 250 pieces, while another has a regular subscription, buying a new piece every month. To keep up with the demand, Weissflog's son, Jakob, assists in the studio, allowing him to continue developing new designs while producing commissioned works.

Jakob has worked in his father's shop since he was young and they decided several years ago that he would begin a formal apprenticeship. After years of taking classes, sitting tests, and producing pieces to prove his technical expertise, Jakob graduated and began working with Hans every day.

More Possibilities in the Lathe

Weissflog carefully plans and perfectly proportions every piece. Weissflog thinks out in advance the steps needed to create the final object. There is no room for error. "I must be totally focused while turning," Weissflog says. "A great many of them break in the process. It's a pity nobody collects only my broken pieces, as it would result in large and interesting collections."

Of his creative process, Weissflog says, "All of the challenges I face influence each other. Everything that happens around me is of some importance. I just have to know what I can use for my work. Normally everything comes together in the end, offering something new I can continue to develop."

Touching Rings Bowl, 1998. Maple; 2¾" high x 10" diameter. "On the outside of the bowl I cut grooves around different centers," Weissflog says. "All the rings have different sizes, causing the outside rings to touch."

ABOVE TOP

Saturn Star Bowl, 2006. Putumuju; 2¾" high x 7" diameter. "*Saturn Star Bowl* is the most complicated piece I've ever made," Weissflog says. "You see the star in the ring and the spider pattern in the middle."

RIGHT TOP

Small Rocking Bowl, 2005. Boxwood, African blackwood; 2½" high x 3¼" wide x 2½" deep. "*Small Rocking Bowl* has the same proportions as the large one and is made from two different kinds of wood, offering a contrast in color.

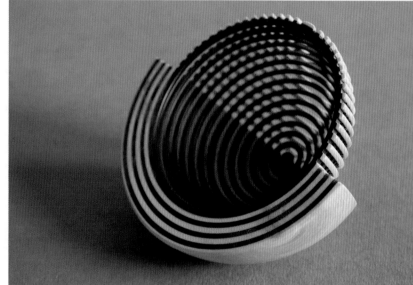

RIGHT BOTTOM

Ball Box, 1994. African blackwood, boxwood; 2" high x 2" diameter. *Ball Box* was one of the forms that initially brought Weissflog international recognition. "I often begin with a sphere," he says. "But this time, rather than adding something, I decided to take something away." What he took away was half the material.

The lathe has proved the best way for Weissflog to express himself. "I believe the lathe provides more possibilities than most people know. That's what I want to show in my designs as it is my most important tool. Everything else in the shop, such as the band saw or grinder, is just to support that work. I would say I spend 85 percent of the day on the lathe. The rest is office work and everything else involved in the business. Once a piece is turned, I don't do any other work on it in the way some artisans carve or paint it."

Weissflog occasionally experiments with other materials such as bone or exotic seeds, but wood remains his ideal material. "Wood is always different," he says. "I own 465 different kinds of wood and they all look, smell, and behave differently, just like humans."

Weissflog has continued to redefine himself, recently exploring the juxtaposition of the raw, organic aspects of wood with the highly controlled, detailed approaches for which he is best known. Weissflog continues to create highly individual works that raise the bar technically and expand the potential of woodturning. It has long been his intention to show the range and complexity of work that can be created on the lathe and he is increasingly interested in showing there are no limitations to the forms that can be turned. It requires careful examination to appreciate his variations on previous designs and complex new works. As he puts it, "I create forms on the border of what it is possible to make."

JACQUES VESERY

When I Get in a Groove, Watch Out

Inspired by Impressionism and the proportional ratios of Fibonacci, Jacques Vesery creates works that don't initially appear to be made of wood at all, yet he finds wood ideal for his sculptural celebrations of the natural world.

When Vesery is asked about his tastes he says, "It's hard for me to separate influence, inspiration, envies, and my tastes. I like so many artists' work. Pisarro, Monet,

When it doesn't feel right, the work is forced and it shows. But when I get in a groove, watch out! I have years and years of good ideas, so many I know I will not get to them all.

Seurat, Cezanne, and Parrish come to mind. Fibonacci and the importance of form, proportion, scale, balance, and perspective is an inspiration."

"I've always been fascinated with the possibilities of wood, even as early as three years old when I hacked a hole in one of my dad's prize Japanese maple trees with a toy axe," Vesery says. "I had done some metal turning in my father's machine shop and experienced woodturning in a seventh-grade shop class. It wasn't until years later, in 1985, that I become truly hooked. I was working as a forest ranger in northern New Jersey and had a workshop space on the property. I was given an old Oliver lathe, which I rebuilt. During the winter months, there was not a lot of work to be done, so it gave me time to play."

ABOVE

Vesery works in his studio at dusk in the Maine winter.

OPPOSITE

Traveling Under Watery Skies, 2005-06. Cherry, acrylic; 6" high x 4" diameter. "Although *Traveling Under Watery Skies* appears sculptural, it is based on a classic form," Vesery says. "By reorienting the form and creating negative space, an illusion occurs, causing the viewer to believe it is from the sea."

Lorelei's Realm, 1995. Curly maple, Macassar ebony, canarywood; 9½" high x 7" diameter. "In my earlier work, I let material and technique drive what I made," Vesery says. "*Lorelei's Realm* connects to my more recent work. Lorelei's Realm was one of a few pieces that grew from form versus material, though not completely."

Vesery moved to Maine in 1990, when his wife, Minda, started a family-practice medicine program in Portland. He initially believed he was going to build furniture part time while he was the stay-at-home dad to their sons, Isaac and Jonah. "I found very quickly that I enjoyed the turning part most and didn't really want to build furniture. I also found turning to be more lucrative at local and regional craft shows. Rarely does a buyer walk away with a bed—but a bowl? Yes."

His service as a submariner, time spent as a scrimshander in Hawaii and Cape Cod, and being a forest ranger all have influenced Vesery's work. By the mid-nineties, he was creating vessels on the lathe, but focusing on segmented turning, using grain and color to enhance the work. "I was frustrated because the materials were driving the forms. The work I was creating could have been anyone's. I also felt a need to put an emphasis on the work rather than the wood."

Creating New Palettes with Every Piece

When he stopped looking at wood as the finished product and started seeing it as a canvas, his work grew substantially, and so did his career. Now the painting is the most exciting aspect of his work. "I get to create new palettes with every piece. When someone looks at one of my pieces, they see a basic color. What they might not realize is there are many layers and at least seven different colors that shift across the piece." Carving and painting the works require an enormous amount of time. "I don't keep track of time and don't price work by time spent," he says. When his wife is asked how much time he puts into his work, she answers, "Countless hours."

Over the years, Vesery has rethought the value of wood as a medium. "If I could make my work more easily or better out of other materials I would, because it's not about the material or method, it's about the outcome. That said, I know wood and I can read it better than other materials. I also am intrigued by how other materials can complement wood, such as when I recently used semi-precious stone as an accent. I guess the bottom line for me is not the importance of wood, but its familiarity. Yet, you don't even know it is wood when you look at most of my work."

While Vesery views the lathe as only a tool, he says, "Quite often it's the right tool for the job. I know the lathe plays a less important role now, but I'll always have a passion for turned forms. I think my work still conveys that, even in the more sculptural pieces."

Winter's First Sister, from the "Pleiades Series," 2006. Cherry, maple burl, holly, gold leaf, acrylic; 6" high x 5" diameter. *Winter's First Sister* is the seventh piece of the Pleiades series, inspired by the constellation also known as the Seven Sisters. "The footless form and feather texture convey a sense of deep unknown space for me," Vesery says.

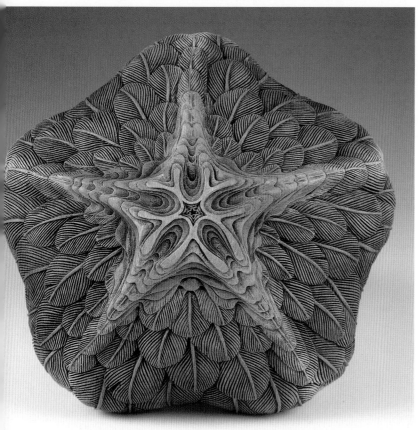

Photo by John Komorowski

ABOVE

Vesery is meticulous in everything he does, including the way he mixes and applies colors.

LEFT

Makana Ka Na Hoku (Gift of the Stars), 2006-07. Cherry, gold leaf, acrylic; 5" wide x 2½" deep. While in the Navy, Vesery sailed out of Pearl Harbor. "It is the place, the people and the sea-life of the Islands that inspired this piece," Vesery says. "My connection to Hawaii is still very strong."

RIGHT

Vesery uses a woodburner for shaping and texturing, not for color. It is the most time consuming part of his work. He colors the entire surface with India ink to even out the ground color, before applying as many as seven layers of acrylic topped by gold leaf.

BELOW

L'ecoulement du Ciel Vers La Mer (The Flow of Sky to Sea), 2007. Cherry, dyed silver leaf, acrylic, blue fluorite; 4" diameter x 2½" deep. "The sea forms I create are near to my heart, more than anything else I have made," Vesery says. "I was born in the water sign Aquarius, my native totem is the sea otter, I was on a submarine in the Navy and I have always lived near the sea."

A Coastal Town in Maine

Vesery and his family reside on the edge of the small coastal town of Damariscotta, Maine, with 2,000 people and a single traffic light installed only a few years ago. They have three acres of mostly wooded land, backed up by three hundred acres of undeveloped forest. "As the crow flies, there is a pond a quarter-mile in front and one a half-mile behind, and the rocky coast is only a few miles away," he says. "It's a great place to raise kids. Folks call our place Camp Jacques and Minda because of the forts in the trees, archery range, a small pond with a waterfall, a log bridge over a stream that leads to hiking trails, and an 18-foot tepee.

The quality of life and the experience of nature are important to Vesery's work. "There was a time when I pooh-poohed the idea of the need to be inspired, or being in the right place or time to be creative," he says. "I thought for so long that you simply work when you need to work. Now I see it is truly not the case. I can go for days not creating a thing. When it doesn't feel right, the work is forced and it shows. But, when I get in a groove, watch out! I have years and years of good ideas, so many I know I will not get to them all.

Photo by John Komorowski

LEFT

A Celadon Sky Dream, 2006. Cherry, gold leaf, acrylic; 5" wide x 2½" deep. "An engaging convergence of color, texture and proportion in any object forms a unique spirit and soul from birth," Vesery says. "Material and technique then become irrelevant."

BELOW TOP

Vesery spends many hours carving, detailing, and painting his creations.

BELOW BOTTOM

Vesery maintains an extraordinarily clean and organized studio. He recently made the space smaller, the better to fit his diminutive work.

That is partly because my techniques take so long, but also because the house stuff, the kids, and the garden easily distract me. It's all right there staring at me, saying 'come water me, weed me, need more color, add some more lilies.' It's a good thing I don't live in Hawaii anymore. Mike Lee and I never would get any work done. We would be surfing all the time."

Despite the temptations to stay outside, Vesery's workspace makes it clear he is a serious artist. "I have a cleaner workshop than most kitchens, lots of light and great views of the woods. I actually made the space a third smaller a few years ago, because creating small work requires less space. Of course, it is organized like a submarine and everything has it place. I do refer to it as a space. It's not quite a studio and not really a shop. It's more of a hardware-store/picture-of-my-life/hangout/make-stuff place."

Photo by John Kornorowski

MICHAEL HOSALUK

I'm Not Afraid to Venture Out of My Comfort Zone

It's hard to describe Michael Hosaluk, because he is so many things—turner, carver, furniture maker, artist, teacher, and inspirer of many other artists. He has created some of the most innovative and challenging pieces to be seen in the field of woodturning, and he has been doing it for many years. He claims it began with

---

Sometimes the work is about the lathe and sometimes the lathe is just the sculpting tool to get close to the finished shape.

---

his life on a small farm: "I was born among people who used their hands. My mother and father always amazed me that amid the everyday life on the farm they would still find time to make things by hand. My mother made crocheting, knitting, and shell art, and my father made furniture we used. He also made aesthetic objects like ships and he showed us how to make crossbows that would knock out the top window of a grain elevator."

Hosaluk has an amazing ability to absorb and use all of the influences that have surrounded him throughout his life. He lists childhood events, family, children, friends, travel, and architecture as just a few of the things that have affected his work. He also acknowledges the "art of unknown artists from ancient cultures whose work lives on in museums." Hosaluk believes the objects "capture the essence of making things by hand and soul. They make us want to make for the love of it, or often the need of it. It is such a good feeling when this happens."

Photo by Jason Hosaluk. Other photos by Grant Kernan unless otherwise indicated.

ABOVE

Hosaluk outside his home in the Saskatchewan winter. "We once had the distinction of being the coldest place on earth for a day!"

OPPOSITE

Scribble, 2005. Ash, acrylic airbrush medium; 15" high x 4½" diameter. Hosaluk is a master of finishes. It would be easy to mistake this for the glazing on a fine ceramic pot, but the glimpse of wood in the interior confirms that it is turned wood. With typical nonchalance, Hosaluk has scribbled circles on the surface, at once both casual and careful.

Home on the Canadian Prairie

Home for Michael Hosaluk is just outside the city of Saskatoon in the Canadian province of Saskatchewan. Hosaluk describes it simply, but poetically: "I live on the prairies. It is like I am surrounded by an ocean of dirt. In the winter, the snow banks resemble sand dunes. If you daydream a bit you can be reminded of beaches, but reality sinks in when you leave the shop and it is still minus-40 degrees outside.

Hosaluk is using the lathe to wind twine onto a wooden frame. Always challenging preconceptions, he describes it as "my latest turning."

Photo by Jason Hosaluk

We once had the distinction of being the coldest place on earth for a day. Come spring and summer, there are oceans of flax that look like water, and the trees and garden are filled with birds."

Hosaluk has been the main force behind the legendary series of collaborative art-making summer camps at Emma Lake in Saskatchewan, and he says all the participants there over the years have inspired him "to reach higher levels in art." Whenever he talks about his work, the talk soon comes around to his friends—and he probably has more than anyone else in the field. "There has been a trail of makers in the furniture/turning field who continue to inspire and influence me. Most importantly, they share their lives. It is a network of friends I will cherish for life and that makes life itself more enjoyable."

A Master of Techniques

Since he began woodworking in 1974, Hosaluk has mastered or invented more techniques than most could dream of. Although he is sometimes described as a turner, like many others in the field today, he finds the word limited. "The lathe is just one of many tools and techniques I use to create my work. Sometimes the work is about the lathe and sometimes the lathe is just the sculpting tool to get close to the finished shape. Compositions of color, form, and content are the most challenging design exercises. I like the interaction of materials and technique, and pushing technical wizardry to take myself to higher levels. I'm not afraid to venture out of my comfort zone and try something completely new because I believe it's our ideas that are most important, not the material. Craft doesn't only deal with aesthetics, but also with our social and ideological lives."

Hosaluk is never limited to established practice. "I love to break rules," he says. "The creative process can produce new technical challenges. The more you open doors to new subject matter, materials and techniques, the greater your vocabulary becomes and your artistic voice can become stronger." Hosaluk's energy is enormous and he seems to jump effortlessly from one idea to the next. "I work on many projects at once. Some things are immediate because

Bird Vase, 2006. Ash, acrylic airbrush medium, 11" high x 4" diameter. It requires many layers of color to achieve a complex image such as this, and yet vestiges of the wood figure still show through. Collaboration with Laura Hosaluk.

Bowl of Strange Fruit. Maple, 2005. Arbutus, birch, acrylic paint, horse and dog hair; 6" high x 4" deep x 24" long. Hosaluk enjoys collaborations, in this case with 12 other artists.

other materials work better for design. Still, just like there are times when the lathe and the tools rule, wood is important to me. I have a reverence for it, I love the immediacy of it, the smell at times, and both the texture it already possesses and that

I believe it's our ideas that are most important, not the material. Craft doesn't only deal with aesthetics, but also with our social and ideological lives.

which I can impose on it. Using it is like alchemy. You can take the plainest wood and transform it into something of great beauty and value. It can make you think in new directions and it comforts me and grounds me when I run out of other ideas."

Hosaluk is one of these rare individuals whose work has been so imitated that many of his innovations are now considered commonplace, but he is typically generous about that. "As a teacher, I accept the fact there will be imitators, but I hope it leads them in new directions. Once you go beyond the materials and begin to express yourself, no one can copy you. That's where the fun starts."

the material and process dictate, but others are a long investigation of a theme or a concept." Hosaluk probably uses more different materials than anyone else in the field. "Wood is the material I am most comfortable with, but there are times when

After turning a hollow form, Hosaluk saws it into three sections so he can remove the middle part, thus changing the round form to something with a narrow spine. To help control the cuts, he has glued the vessel to a board.

After flattening the edges of the pieces on a belt sander, Hosaluk joins them together with yellow glue, binding them with strips of rubber until the glue dries.

Hosaluk sands the edges of the join, then drills small holes to receive the spines, which are made from toothpicks.

Next Hosaluk glues on the fins made from rice paper, and paints them with acrylic gel to add strength and make them translucent.

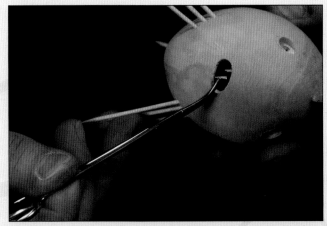

After carving the mouth of the fish, Hosaluk glues in teeth he made from the ends of toothpicks. The eyes also have been drilled.

Untitled, 2002. Maple and birch, 4" to 6" high x 2" to 4" wide x 5" to 8" long. A few coats of acrylic paint and the fish are finished.

MICHAEL MODE

The Intimate Interplay of Idea, Hand, and Eye

Michael Mode lived in Kashmir for a year in the early 1970s and was influenced by the artists and craftsmen he saw there. The impact of their work remains important: "They possess a strong tradition of art and craft, much of it derived from Persia, and their patient, meticulous work inspired me to go much further in creative endeavors than I ever had at that point."

Back in the United States, Mode's woodworking career began with simple carpentry, construction work, and cabinetry. When he assembled a harpsichord kit in 1975, he experienced how careful fitting of parts, sturdy construction, and finish could result in a beautiful object. That same year, he made a foot-powered lathe using an old sewing machine treadle and assorted parts. "I didn't know a single soul who turned wood, but I once observed a man in Morocco using a bow lathe and it caught my fancy. I read one book and made primitive

---

I began knowing nothing, and was very tentative and private. Today, I have a large amount of confidence in my work, and the wonderful fluidity and fluency of technique makes the creative process very sweet.

---

tools." Mode was 29-years-old the first time he tried turning on his homemade lathe. "Somehow, everything clicked. The part of my life I now label 'creative explorations' came to an end, to be replaced by 'creative expressions,' still continuing."

ABOVE
Mode turns a large form made up of laminated blocks of contrasting woods.

OPPOSITE
Zebra Rising, 2004. Wenge, holly, koa; 5¾" high x 8½" diameter. The title of the bowl, an exploration of complexity and serendipity, reflects the black-and-white patterning on a zebra.

Intersections, 1999. Purpleheart, holly, wenge, ebony, pink ivory wood; 11" high x 8½" diameter. "Lidded vessels were my primary object from the beginning of my turning focus in 1975 until the spring 1999, when I became interested in the stack lamination process of bowl making," Mode says.

Intricate and Colorful Laminated Vessels

Throughout the 1980s, Michael Mode created lidded vessels from burls and spalted wood. In the early '90s, his work changed substantially, ranging from miniature chess sets fitted within lidded vessels, to architecturally inspired domed and winged forms reminiscent of the Mughal buildings he saw in India. The Islamic inspiration led to a series of laminated vessels of colorful and intricate design with seemingly infinite varieties of color and pattern.

Mode's continuing love of wood as a medium is due to, as he says, "the fact that wood comes from a living organism and carries something of that life within itself, with all the variegated beauty that entails. The marvelous workability of wood, its rich history in our lives and culture, my lifelong relationship with trees and forests, the sheer sensuality of working with wood and the variety of species available all define my preference for the material."

Apart from the material, Mode also values the level of expertise he has achieved.

Within six months, Mode had replaced his foot-powered lathe with a motorized one, later replaced by a succession of better lathes and equipment. David Ellsworth (page xi) provided early inspiration on many levels. When the two met in 1981, Ellsworth showed Mode the array of burls and exotic woods available. He also explained important aspects of doing business in the craft world. Most importantly, Ellsworth proved that one could make a living as a lathe artist.

Summer Madness Abacus, 2004. Various woods; 35" high x 60" wide. "The abacus idea began as a request from a good client who wanted a very large wall-mounted abacus for his living room," Mode explains. "The piece turned out wonderfully and I've had others commissioned, resulting in a series of six abacuses so far."

LEFT

Slow Roll, 2005. Ziricote, wenge, purpleheart, kingwood, pink ivory wood; 6½" high x 11¾" diameter. Often it is simply the beauty of the wood that motivates me," Mode says. "In this case, the ziricote amplified by the color of pink ivory wood and kingwood kept me going."

BELOW

Of Many Hands, 2005. Wenge, mahogany, pink ivory wood, purpleheart; 9" high x 15¾" diameter. A signature design represents Mode's entire bowl-making period.

Walking Cathedrals, 2006. Honduras rosewood, mahogany; 10" high. An exploration of the checkerboard design pushes the limits of thinness in a sculptural form.

Boat of Babel, 2006. Lacewood, holly, whalebone; 8" high x 8" wide x 32" deep. "The pattern reminds me of an Arabic script called kufic, each line of which is stating something different at the same time."

"I value the skill levels I have acquired during thirty-one years of turning, mostly because there is now little impediment between the conception of an object and the fluent creation of it. I often compare woodturning to playing a piano: years of practice are required to play a Beethoven sonata, but an accomplished player can perform a piece with a blissful ease. That said, my pursuit of the expression of inspirations sometimes leads to an unfamiliar technical area requiring new skills. I relish those challenges as they increase my vocabulary. My inspirations and designs do tend to flow into the channels created by the skills I possess. Rarely do I create something requiring me to start from scratch with new techniques. I began knowing nothing, and was very tentative and private. Today, I have a large amount of confidence in my work, and the wonderful fluidity and fluency of technique makes the creative process very sweet."

Mode still has a strong love of the lathe itself. "I love the spontaneous immediacy of lathe work and the intimate interplay of idea, hand and eye. Because of the closeness with the machine and its techniques, my work generally has a turned look. In my earlier work, I did nearly everything on the lathe. Most of my current work is laminated to some extent, even to a high degree, so I might spend more than 50 percent of my time planning, cutting, machining, and gluing a piece. Sometimes I use the lathe only to perfect the form that was already shaped in other ways. Most of my pieces are finished on the lathe."

MY ASIAN NOMAD LATHE

While perusing a book entitled Nomads of Central Asia, I came across a photo of a man and his wife from Kyrgyzstan making a bowl on a simple hand powered reciprocating lathe. I liked the possibility of making one myself, I called Will Wallace/Gusakov, a young friend and turning enthusiast, and on a morning in May 2005, we put together the lathe shown in the woods. We made one small bowl in the afternoon. Most of the parts could be made with an axe out of a log and some branches. The mounting spindle or mandrel and the turning tools would be the only thing the nomad needed to carry to be capable of making wooden dishware.

I have always thought that knowing the roots of a craft, of how it was done in the old days, is important to my understanding and appreciation of what was done before, in most cases without all of the technology available today.

—Michael Mode

Views of the Adirondacks

Michael Mode's home and studio are located in Vermont's Lake Champlain valley, with spectacular views of the Adirondack Mountains to the west and the foothills of the Green Mountains to the east. The yard frequently is visited by wildlife, including deer, wild turkeys, bobcats, coyotes, and rabbits. "We are comfortably secluded on ten acres, mostly wooded, with a three-quarter-mile driveway," Mode says. "I travel a lot to market my work, and each time I return home, I realize again the many blessings of living in this very special place." Mode's wife, Lynn Yarrington, designs and hand-weaves fabrics, producing a unique and beautiful line of women's clothing. The two maintain separate studios in the same building on their property

Over the years, Mode has seen tremendous growth in the field of woodturning. "To me it seems like a slow-motion explosion of talent and creativity, with so many artists doing unique and exciting work. Every time I attend an exhibition or see a book of turning, it blows me away." He also has found the public is much more perceptive about wood than they were in the past. While his work is featured in leading galleries, the majority of Mode's work is sold to individuals who do not think of themselves as collectors. He finds many of his customers at art fairs. "Sending work to a gallery and receiving a check a few months later can be kind of lonely. I really enjoy meeting and interacting with clients, and hearing their reactions. Often someone tells me the piece they bought four years ago sits on their entryway table and seeing it each day makes them feel good. That makes me feel good."

ABOVE TOP
Mode lives near Bristol in Vermont's Lake Champlain Valley, with spectacular views of the Adirondack Mountains.

ABOVE BOTTOM
Mode shares a studio building with his wife, fiber artist Lynn Yarrington.

After experimenting with ring-cutting techniques, Mode became intrigued by the process. "I had to overcome my 25-year-old urge to put a lid on whatever I made," he says. "Then the bowl making took over my creative output almost entirely. I like the process for two major reasons: It's a remarkably efficient way of using wood, and it opens up a huge design space different from anything else I've done."

Mode is going to make a laminated ring-cut bowl like this.

The artist begins by selecting strips of wood and making a pleasing arrangement.

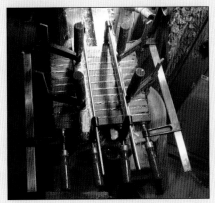

Mode glues the strips together, with extra clamps to keep them flat.

Mode machines a long bevel on the blank, and glues on a wedge of light-colored wood.

Mode goes to the lathe to cut the disk into a series of concentric rings with sloping sides.

He stacks the rings and glues them into a bowl-shaped blank with the center already hollowed.

Mode mounts the stacked blank on the lathe and refines the bowl.

DEWEY GARRETT

The Lathe Places a Limit, Yet Offers Endless Possibilities

Dewey Garrett was born to be a woodworker. His parents made most of their furniture in a basement workshop before he was born. His mother specialized in turning legs and other furniture parts, and she also made lamps, salad bowls, and a number of wall sconces using split turnings. After college, where he studied engineering, Garrett found himself dreaming about making things. He would satisfy his desire by going to the library for books on woodworking and tools, dreaming of the day he would have a workshop.

When a new job took Garrett to northern California, he bought a house with a garage and started buying tools, scouting yard sales for everything he needed. "I'm frugal by nature and try to make tools, or adapt them to fit," he says. "I purchased a lathe with a metal frame, cut the frame in half, then enclosed and strengthened it with a wood and plywood outer shell. I relocated the motor to the inside of the frame and added a jackshaft to lower the speed ranges. After using it for a couple of years, I replaced the motor and added a controller. When I encounter a limitation, I remember that old saw: 'It's a poor workman who blames his tools.'"

Soon after creating his garage shop, Garrett was making furniture

All photos courtesy the artist unless otherwise indicated

ABOVE

Garrett trims a block of palm to prepare it for turning. The wood is rough and fibrous—exactly what he wants.

LEFT

Palm trees abound in northern California where Garrett lives, so he has been discovering ways to work with the fibrous wood.

OPPOSITE

Stories, 2005. Ebonized oak, metalized acrylics, patinas; 14½" high x 13½" diameter. "*Stories* is made of turned segments aged with patinas and situated by levels on a tower," Garrett says. "The levels—stories—suggest an unfinished construction of unknown purpose, started and abandoned."

too good for the furniture he had planned to make. Instead he turned a platter and saw that there was tremendous potential in turning objects. He set out looking for wood, books, and inspiration, and was soon turning bowls and platters in exotic woods including purpleheart, koa, and zebrawood. After turning green wood from a neighbor's firewood, Garrett was hooked forever by the thrill of the experience, going on to create a

---

A single operator mistake can ruin the piece or crash the machine. Mental lapses and programming errors can ruin a piece in a fraction of a second.

---

range of turned work, but never completing the furniture he had been planning to make.

Early on, magazine photos of bowls and vessels by many other woodturners inspired Garrett. "I believe their work was important in setting challenging standards for turned work. Robyn Horn's early work showed me how simple turnings could become expressive and sculptural. It all opened my eyes to possibilities I had never imagined."

Garrett resides and works in Livermore, California, in a valley about 40 miles east of San Francisco. "My town has many trees common to American neighborhoods and nearby valleys have orchards of pecan, walnut and apricot. The climate here supports palm trees and I've been fortunate to get wood from some of them."

A B O V E

White City, 2006. Bleached oak; 6" high x 14" diameter. Garrett assembled *White City*, and others in his City Series, from many small turned, sawn, and drilled blocks of wood. Bleaching the oak de-emphasizes the wood figure.

R I G H T

Impact Grid, 2006. Bleached oak; 11½" high x 11½" wide x 4" diameter. "In these pieces, I've continued my exploration of bowl forms embedded in a block but tried to make a stronger effect with the larger block components," Garrett says.

for his new home and needed to use a lathe to make a stool. With some turning experience as a youth on his parents' Sears lathe, he sharpened a set of chisels and began to turn. When a load of old walnut lumber arrived from Missouri, he realized the beautiful flame-figured crotch wood was

Lamination and Negative Space

Garrett soon began using lamination and negative space to create sculptural vessels. His previous bowls and platters had showcased the natural wood, but he found the wood figure now disturbed the strength of the curved lines. After bleaching or ebonizing, the wood grain became less obvious, leading to a stronger visual statement. "I had just a few years' experience turning when these ideas came to me," Garrett said. "I had a picture in my mind of what I wanted the forms to look like and how it would expose the structure and interplay of space and material. Little did I know what a difficult project I was starting. It took numerous tries and failures to develop the methods of construction. The failures were spectacular and scary—simple and instantaneous disassemblies." By the time Garrett had successfully created the first in the series, he had ideas for others. "I wanted to explore different shapes and ratios. I experimented with the spacing of the material and the intervening space. These led to pieces with no rim and only a skeleton framework."

Design and problem solving are an important part of the creative process for Garrett. "I spend a lot of time making drawings in a notebook. I also spend many evenings writing software to create patterns or improve the operation of my equipment. I'm always surprised to see the design take shape in the shop after trying to visualize it in my mind and in two-dimensions on paper."

Garrett finds the lathe is a much-needed constraint on design. "The mind can envision so much and I can't possibly follow every idea, so the lathe places a limit, yet still offers seemingly endless possibilities. I have to deal with the inherent symmetry and decide how to incorporate that into the design. As an engineer, I learned there are many solutions to most problems." Although the lathe is central to Garrett's work, he spends a lot of time gluing up segments, or milling and assembling gridded frames. After turning the form, he spends more time painting, final sanding, and cleaning up.

Garrett learned to create a number of patinas by applying acrylic paints loaded with tiny metal particles and applying acids while wet to create a chemical reaction. The process is very rapid and the colors are locked into the drying finish. "I like the

BELOW TOP

Exploration, 1992. Maple & padauk; 4" high x 14" diameter. Garrett learned a great deal making these forms, and once done he also discovered the moiré effect of apparent motion, to a moving viewer, of an unmoving object.

BELOW BOTTOM

Analysis #1, 1992. Alder and padauk; 3½" high x 12" diameter. Garrett experimented with numerous alternative designs investigating the effects of combining the open forms with their solid counterparts.

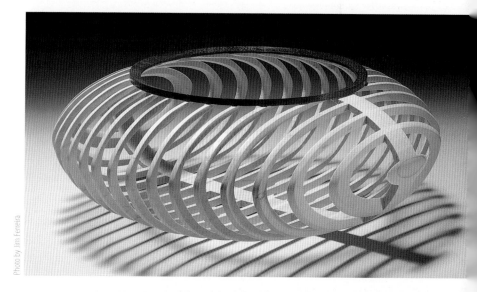

Photo by Jim Ferreira

Rediscovering Ornamental Turning

After retiring from his engineering career, Garrett wanted technical challenges because he enjoyed solving engineering problems, mathematics, and software design. Garret's desire for technical challenges led him to ornamental woodturning, which he saw demonstrated at a symposium. While he had been aware of ornamental turning, he had never seen a machine in action. The demonstration of the simplicity of the rocking mechanism of a rose engine and the complex patterns it produced were fascinating. "It immediately occurred to me I could make a simple machine with few moving parts using stepper motors and linear motion translation stages," Garrett says. "The complex motion produced by a rose engine could be emulated quite simply by applying basic equations to the motions of a transverse axis. The indexing could be accomplished by stepped motion of a single rotary axis; traverse along the length of a piece required motion along a longitudinal axis."

Photo by Jim Ferreira

Garrett began to acquire the components for the machine and to write software to control it. He merged it with an open-source machine controller project originally developed by engineers at the National Institute of Standards and Technology. The fascinating and challenging process instantly captured his attention. "I've already discovered that while I began the design to emulate a rose engine, I can make patterns conventionally produced by eccentric cutting and other engine mechanisms too. I have found the machine is very demanding

ABOVE TOP

Gridded Cone. Bleached oak, 7" high x 14" wide x 14" deep. In *Gridded Cone*, Garrett placed the remnants of the bowl form at the center of wooden slats. The view changes as the observer moves around the piece.

ABOVE BOTTOM

LIM #3, 1993. Bleached maple, padauk; 4" high x 12" diameter. Garrett's explorations led to works with no rim and only a skeleton framework remaining. "I named these LIM, from the idea that less is more expressed by Mies van der Rohe," Garrett notes. "After that, I decided I was finished with the series."

aged, metallic look and find it interesting when a strong wood grain is still visible through the finish," he said.

Although Garrett occasionally works in other materials, including plastics, he has a great attachment to wood. "I grew up with a woodworking tradition, so wood has always been familiar to me. I like the smell of freshly cut wood and the fact it can be worked with simple, accessible tools. The satisfaction and speed of making bowls on the lathe continues to be enjoyable. I like the simplicity of the tool, the feel and sound of the cutting, the symmetry of form, and the myriad possibilities for design. I also respect the place of the tool in history and civilization.

and unforgiving of error—to a much greater extent than conventional turning. The precision requires special care and setup of the equipment and introduces a myriad of possibilities for human error. During

---

I spend a lot of time making drawings in a notebook, and writing software to create patterns or improve the operation of my equipment. I'm always surprised to see the design take shape in the shop after trying to visualize it in my mind and on paper.

---

setup, the part must be jogged in each axis to center it, and a single operator mistake can ruin the piece or crash the machine, necessitating realignment. Moreover, mental lapses and programming errors can ruin a piece in a fraction of a second. I confess to having made many errors but I do think the results will eventually offset the humbling learning experience."

Photo by Jim Ferreira

ABOVE TOP

Visitors, 1996. Ebonized walnut, 8" high x 8" diameter. The intricate pieces are built up with an interior design and then turned to a sphere, carved, and opened to reveal the structure inside.

ABOVE BOTTOM

Untitled Box, 2006. Alternative ivory, celluloid abalone; 3" high. "After building an ornamental turning machine, I began making simple boxes with delicate geometrical patterns," Garrett says. "The modern synthetic materials have excellent machining properties critical in this type of work."

Using scientific lab equipment and ingenuity, Garrett devised an apparatus for duplicating ornamental turnings. In operation, it steers the workpiece against a powered cutter on a precisely controlled, multi-axis path.

In contrast to his assembled pieces, Garrett's Palm Vessels Series requires an immediate process. Garrett chainsaws the wood into a block, turns it, and then sets it aside for some months to dry. The palm vessels later require numerous applications of bleach, followed by several applications of dye, before they can be finished with Danish oil.

Tree cutters fell palm trees, creating a trove of fresh material for Garrett to work with.

Conventional turning converts the palm block into a vessel form.

Garrett bores a center hole, to begin turning the inside of the palm block and also to gauge its depth.

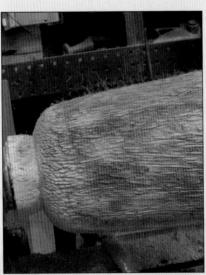

Garrett works over the palm wood with a stiff wire brush, creating the rough texture he prefers.

Garrett bleaches the bland palm wood, and then paints it with intense dyes, which soak deep into the fibrous material.

ABOVE TOP

Pitted Palm Bowl, 2006. Dyed palm; 3¼" high x 13¼" diameter. After turning about a thousand pounds of palm wood, I began to experiment with simple carvings using a rotary burr," Garrett says. "I liked the way the spherical cuts interact with the fibers of the wood."

ABOVE BOTTOM

Palm Vessel with Beads, 2006. Dyed palm; 13" diameter. One winter when it was too cold to turn, Garrett experimented with beads to highlight and intensify the simple carvings in the palm wood.

www.deweygarrett.com

BETTY SCARPINO

It's Like Discovering Hidden Treasure

Betty Scarpino's early life didn't really offer any clues to how she would become an artist working in wood. "Although there were no role models within my family or in my early years of life, as I grew up I had the freedom to explore. Reading the biographies and seeing the work of women artists, such as Georgia O'Keeffe, Louise Nevelson, Beatrice Potter, and Barbara Hepworth, helped me understand what it takes to be an artist. Because I could identify with them, I could envision a career for myself in the world of art."

Her involvement with art began around thirty years ago when she took a woodworking class at the University of Missouri. She says that at that time, she had no clue where it would lead, but, "I knew I enjoyed making things and when I was working with my hands I was happy." Scarpino ended up with a degree in industrial arts with a specialty in woodworking, along with a number of inspirational classes in the art department.

Great Light in Indianapolis

Scarpino's home is in a quiet neighborhood of Indianapolis and her studio is a one-car garage that boasts a skylight, a large window, and plenty of insulation. When the weather permits, she can open the garage door, the back door, and the window. "It's like being outdoors, I love the abundance of light. I painted the walls white and the floor various shades of pink in a swirl pattern. Of course, most visitors only notice

All photos by Shawn Spence

ABOVE

In a meditative state, Scarpino outlines ideas directly onto the wood. She can spend hours musing on her designs, working intuitively.

OPPOSITE

Disobedient Currents, 2007. Maple, turned and carved, bleached and painted, stippled, textured; 18" diameter; walnut stand is 15" long. *Disobedient Currents* is from Scarpino's Altered Plates Series. She transforms a turned disc into something very complex, while retaining the simple lines of the original turning.

OPPOSITE INSET

Disobedient Currents, 2007. Reverse side.

Scarpino turns a disk that she will extensively rework, by carving, sanding, and painting, into one of her sculptures.

Double Entendre, 2007. Maple, turned, cut, carved, 15" diameter, 3½" thick. *Double Entendre* is a typical example of Scarpino's interactive sculptures. By rearranging the pieces and changing the distance between them, different feelings of closeness, aloofness, dependency, or independence can be evoked. *Double Entendre* was sawn from one turned disk.

the heaps of wood shavings littering the floor." Although much of her work begins on the lathe, Scarpino spends a lot of time sitting at her workbench in front of the large window, where she does most of her carving, sanding, texturing, and coloring.

For Scarpino, creating wood art is a continuing adventure. "I love the feeling of anticipation when I first walk into my studio. All of my subjects await me: lathe, wood, tools, projects, and ideas. I might carve or sand all day on one project, or I might start something new. For some of my work, I begin a sculpture with a turned plate or a disc. My time at the lathe is minimal and the real involvement happens when I start to carve. The initial cuts are messy and sometimes I believe I have ruined something already lovely. However, I usually end up with a new, more splendid creation, something I am much closer to than the original turning. It's how we live our lives, altering what already exists, revealing new aspects of our complex natures."

Along with many wood artists who use the lathe, Scarpino has a long history as a turner. Through the 1980s, she produced functional items such as cutting boards, candle holders, and bowls. Although the work honed her skills, it was not as satisfying as she wanted. "I don't want to denigrate production work, but it is so boring sometimes. Still, I'm

I like to discover what lies below the surface, within a turned form.

using the techniques I learned during that time for my one-off work now." During the 1990s, when the trend to carve work off the lathe came into fashion, Scarpino's carving background came to the fore. "I embrace the limitations of the lathe by making turned forms and altering them to create sculpture. The lathe is bound up in tradition and technically structured, round items are the usual outcome. I like to discover what lies below the surface, within a turned form. It's like discovering hidden treasure."

LEFT

Undercurrent, 2005. Maple, bleach; 13" diameter. Another of the *Altered Plate* series. Bleaching the wood highlights the deeper natural wood tones of the carved potion.

BELOW LEFT

Using a variety of carving tools, from power carvers to traditional gouges, Scarpino brings her ideas into three-dimensional relief. Here, she is carving *Undercurrent*.

BELOW RIGHT

Scarpino spends hours sanding her work to the fine degree of finish she requires, working her way through many grades of sandpaper until it satisfies her. She does not hesitate to start over if the result does not meet her exacting requirements.

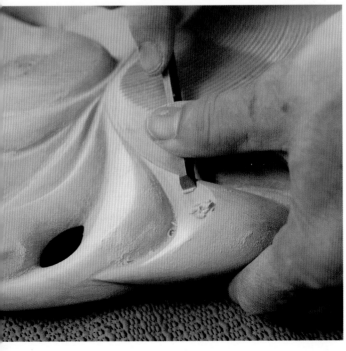

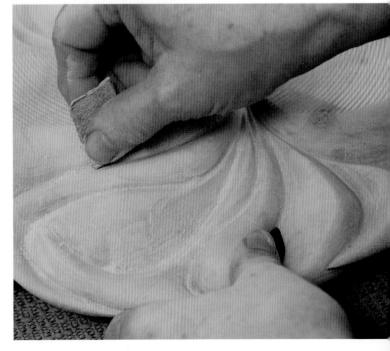

First Journey, 2005. Ash, stain, liming wax, 44" x 8" x 3". Many of Scarpino's sculptures, in her words, "depict feminine themes, while at the same time, they stand for universal ideas." The only turned elements are the eggs.

Scarpino rubs back liming wax that has been colored with yellow/gold pigment. Her repertoire of finishing and coloring techniques is very sophisticated.

An Intuitive Process

Once Scarpino starts to carve, it is a very intuitive process. "I almost never plan or draw a carved form, although I sometimes draw on the wood. Then, as I carve the wood, it's just like playing. I take my time and let the design evolve. I've never been able to draw well, which is OK, because I think clearly in three dimensions." The initial turning may be done in a few hours, but the subsequent carving can take days or even weeks. Scarpino uses a combination of power and hand tools, followed by some power sanding.

The final sanding is where Scarpino's perfectionist temperament shows. She is prepared to work methodically and sand by hand until the finish is as silky as she wants. If the result is not perfect, she is prepared to go back and do it again. The final surface is so well finished that often only a single coat of Danish oil is needed. Scarpino mounts many of her sculptures on integral stands. They are often painstakingly hand carved, then finished to the same fine level as the rest of the sculpture.

Scarpino has developed a high profile as a wood artist by building on the basic elements of the turned form and transforming it into sculpture. She retains enough of the evidence of turning in each piece to both acknowledge and deny it is turned work. Those who are not familiar with the world of turned wood may see her work as purely sculpture using some unusual techniques. Those who are familiar with turned wood art see it is turning

taken to new heights. Part of the intrigue is to unravel the steps Scarpino has taken to transform a basic turned shape into something that is at once blindingly simple and extremely complex.

As Scarpino explains, a lot of her work involves exploring limits, which gives us a small clue to the life experiences that have

I embrace the limitations of the lathe by making turned forms and altering them to create sculpture.

shaped her attitudes to her art. She often talks of "breaking out" or "opening up." As she says, "Limits demand a creative approach. How can I do what I do and keep it within the boundaries of the theme or idea? I am often deadline-oriented and I almost always ship finished sculptures on time. Deadlines provide structure and so do exhibitions with themes."

Any tool that does the job is acceptable to Scarpino. "I use the bandsaw for some initial, major cuts, and whenever possible to remove wood. Other tools in my arsenal include grinders, reciprocating and rotary carvers, rasps and sanding discs. In other words, anything that will quickly remove wood is fair game. Over the years, one of the challenges I faced was a fear of trying new things. My journey to working on a larger scale and more quickly was a long, slow process. My willingness to try color also was slow to take hold. I don't regret the slowness. All the while I was living my life, figuring out what kind of person I am and want to be. That in itself is a slow process. These things take time."

www.bettyscarpino.com

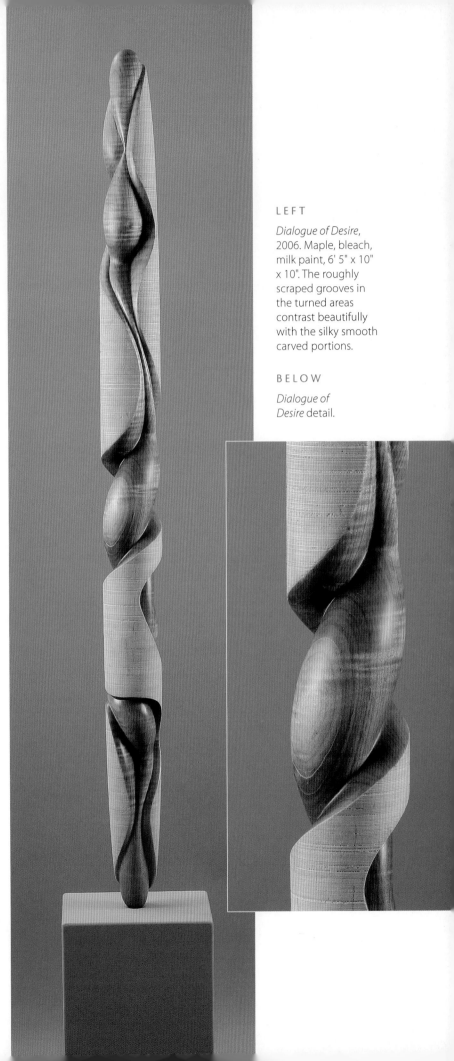

CHRISTOPHE NANCEY

A Symbolic Picture of the Living Process

Christophe Nancey beautifully describes where he resides in the Burgundy region in the middle of France: "I live in green countryside with plenty of forests, fields of wheat, sunflowers, cows, and, of course, vineyards. The area has a wonderful history with many cathedrals, castles, and ancient towns. Many artists

---

It's a very quiet place and most of the people are farmers, so the presence of nature strongly affects daily life.

---

and craftspeople live here, too. I live and work in a very small village called Château du Bois, which means 'wood castle.' Around one hundred people live in my village. I have just started to restore a nineteenth century stone farmhouse and the workshop is in an old barn that opens onto a large orchard. It's a very quiet place and most of the people are farmers, so the presence of nature strongly affects daily life."

Nancey's father was a cabinet maker and he worked with wood from the age of 14. He first saw woodturning when he was 12. "My mother was an antique dealer and she showed me a little wooden box, hollow and curved inside. I asked my father how it was done, but he didn't know. I kept the box. Ten years later, I was helping my father with some furniture repairs and there were some turned parts that needed fixing. I did a short course on traditional turning, and then I realized how the box was made."

All photos courtesy the artist unless otherwise indicated

ABOVE

Nancey pauses while carving in his workshop.

OPPOSITE

Under the sign of Pi, 1997, Ash burl, pewter, steel; 82½" high. *Under the sign of Pi*, a monumental piece, is actually many pieces in one: falling teardrop, suspended vessel, and framed artwork. Rarely is a hollow wooden vessel used so creatively.

Nancey's workshop is in a 200-year-old barn next to his farmhouse home in the Burgundy village of Château du Bois.

Nancey soon saw wood turning held more potential for him than reproduction work. "I was sure I had discovered a very powerful artistic medium and immediately thought, 'That's what I want to do.' During the following years I worked to improve my knowledge, largely on my own." Working alone was common among French turners at the time as they had yet to tap into the world turning revival and had no national bodies to introduce them to each other. "I developed my own techniques of cutting, burning, painting, coloring, segmenting, texturing, inlaying… During the eighties, I worked toward creating my own style of work. In the nineties I focused on inlaying pewter in the natural cracks in burls. I also created a technique to build hollow shapes made from mosaics of pieces of natural-edged wood linked by pewter or wire."

Once the turning is done, Nancey aggressively attacks the piece with a power carving tool.

Expanding Horizons

Around the mid-90s, French turners had started to participate in the international field of turning and the legendary conferences later organized by Jean-Francois Escoulen galvanized the French turning community. Nancey was one of those who expanded his horizons immensely during the period. "I learnt the techniques of deep hollowing and expanded my view by participating in workshops and seminars. I also traveled to the United States."

Now Nancey believes he has settled into a kind of artistic maturity, confident in his repertoire of techniques and his ability to express his ideas. "Since 2000, I have been using more and more carving

---

The woods are mainly roots and burls. I had to learn how to read the wood, what will happen while drying, what I will discover inside.

---

techniques and I can explore my ideas with the benefit of twenty years of experience. Wood turning is only one of the techniques I use. Generally, pieces are first shaped and hollowed on the lathe, and this defines the volume in which I will express the idea. It is the first reading of the piece of wood. Next, I may use different carving and finishing processes. Even though it is an essential step, in most of my pieces, I turn for only 10 percent to 20 percent of the workshop time. Most of the time is spent on carving, texturing, pigmenting, inlaying, finishing…. I suppose I have moved beyond simple woodturning and have become a wood artist."

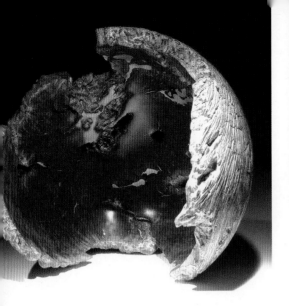

Nancey's work clearly expresses his empathy with nature. "When I make a piece, I try creating a symbolic picture of the living process. Some pieces appear to be natural objects found in an imaginary forest, such as seeds and seed pods. Other pieces are like the eroded aftermath of natural events that occurred in the distant past, but which are still surviving. I like to create the impression that they were found as they are, but of course they weren't. I carefully turn and carve them using not only wood, but pewter inlay, texturing, and pigments, to create the desired effect. The main challenge I have to face during a day of work is to be free of the limits of technique so I can focus on finding the best balance and the strongest expression for the piece I'm making."

ABOVE RIGHT

Cocoon, 2003. Manzanita, pewter, pigments; turned, carved and textured; 19½" long. Some of Nancey's pieces appear to be natural objects found in an imaginary forest.

ABOVE LEFT

Fragment, 2004. Manzanita, pewter, pigments; turned and textured; 13½" diameter. Some pieces are like the eroded aftermath of natural events that occurred in the distant past, but which still persist.

RIGHT

The Guardians, 2004. Heather root, pewter, pigments; turned on two axes, carved and textured; heights 7¾" and 9½". The solid forms seem like alien life. It is quite difficult to turn simple shapes like this, because the protruding part has to be turned separately from the main body, before it can be carved.

Horizon, 2007. Elm burl, pewter, pigments; turned inside, carved and textured; 29½" high. In *Horizon*, Nancey has taken the turned form into the realm of sculpture. As he says: "The main challenge I have to face during a day of work is to be free of the limits of technique so I can focus on finding the best balance and the strongest expression for the piece I'm making."

Reading the Wood

Despite his wish to rise above the limits of technique, Nancey acknowledges practical considerations. "The strongest challenge I had in the past was to learn to read the wood, what will happen while drying, what

I like to create the impression they were found as they are, but of course they weren't. I carefully turn and carve them using not only wood, but pewter inlay, texturing, and pigments…

I will discover inside. The woods I use are mainly roots and burls. Very often I start with green wood, dry the rough shape and then finish the work. I sometimes incorporate the natural changes in the shape, but sometimes I remove them, according to the result I want. I see the

wood as my first tool and my first source of inspiration. When it grows, each tree creates different grain and patterns. This gives every tree and piece of wood different physical and aesthetic properties. When it dries, it moves, cracks and changes the shape I've created. It is a living material. I like to say I work with wood."

Apart from the powerful influence of nature, Nancey also says he has admired many artists who have nourished his ideas. "Apart from the Renaissance, Impressionist, and Modern masters, the strongest emotion I have experienced was from the paintings of Michael Barcelo. In the wood art field, David Ellsworth (page xi) and David Nash have been important, but also Andy Goldsworthy and many others. I also feel very strongly about ethnic and primitive art," Nancy said. All of these influences combine in the work of a genial man. His enthusiasm never seems to wane and we are all the richer for it.

ABOVE

Seed, 2006. Heather root, pewter, pigment; turned, carved and textured; 13" diameter. Nancey strives to persuade viewers his sculptures were found just as they are.

LEFT

Hollow form, 2001, Manzanita, pewter; 9½" high. Hollow form is reminiscent of the natural-edged work popular in the 1980s, but Nancey has made it his own with the subtle pewter inlay.

Photo by Roger Smith

VIRGINIA DOTSON

Shaping Layered Wood Reveals Compositions of Patterns

Raised in a family of musicians, Virginia Dotson credits her early immersion in, and her ongoing enjoyment of, music as a major influence in her work. However, it is nature that has had the greatest impact. As a child,

---

I like to work in series of related pieces to explore a theme more fully.

---

she spent countless hours exploring the woods near her house, and summer trips to the beaches and mountains were further opportunities to explore the natural world. It would take decades, however, before she discovered the means of exploring these early influences in woodturning.

"I didn't find a direct path to woodturning," Dotson says. She started working with furniture, restoring antiques, and later learning other furniture techniques including bent-lamination and stacked-lamination. While studying for her bachelor of fine arts degree at Arizona State University, she was exposed to contemporary furniture and to woodturning, and they both initially appealed to her.

"Three artists directly influenced my work at the very beginning," Dotson recalls. "Wendell Castle's stack-laminated functional pieces transformed the very concept of furniture, while Bob Stocksdale's exquisite vessels served as examples of perfect pitch in visual terms. The early plywood vessels of Rudy Osolnik showed a common material could indeed become a beautiful object."

All photos courtesy the artist

ABOVE

Dotson, shown here under a rock overhang in Canyon de Chelly, draws much inspiration from the layered landscape of the Arizona desert.

OPPOSITE

Sunlight Series #22, 2004. Curly birch and ebonized walnut, 9¼" high x 7¼" diameter. Dotson says the layers of wood echo "layered forms I have observed in nature, like the sedimentary rock landscapes common in the Southwestern United States where I live. Their history is recorded among the layers."

Exploring Many Ideas

Woodturning offered Dotson the opportunity to explore stack-laminating techniques, while its limited scale allowed her to develop a concept by working quickly through ideas. "The activity of working generates more ideas for new work," Dotson says of her process. "I may do brief sketches of ideas as they occur, or test new combinations of materials. When some of them coalesce into a more definite form, I start in. I like to work in series of related pieces to explore a theme more fully. Sometimes, I revisit an earlier series later on. At any given time, I may be working on pieces from a few different groups. If I need

to set one aside before continuing, I can work on another of the pieces."

Virginia Dotson's work is very much tied to the material. "I love the great variety of patterns formed by the growth rings of wood," she says. "Even plain wood exhibits its history in an interesting way when it is shaped to one curve or another. The layers in the hardwood plywood I use can mimic the patterns. The features add a richness that sets wood apart from other materials. Sometimes, I find interesting interactions between the wood figure and the patterns I have created by layering different woods together."

Dotson uses a variety of tools in her work, but it is the lathe that ties everything together. "Turning by itself is not usually the major time commitment in my work. Depending on the piece, there may be a lot of up-front work preparing the materials and gluing up blanks. At the other end of the process, carving out a spiral or other pattern from a turned shell may easily take more time than the turning. Sculpture compositions often require parts that are made by other means than turning."

Inspired by Layers

The natural layering of wood grain and her imitation of it with laminated plywood inspire Dotson. The layers also remind her of the sedimentary rock landscapes in deserts, and the connection continues to inspire her. For many years, she resided in the low desert on the edge of Phoenix, Arizona, an environment that greatly influenced her work. Her laminated vessels translate the southwestern landscape, the layers of rock, light, and shadow, and the lines that run through it all. Recently, she moved to a highly elevated forested region near a small community. "I am now closer to some of the natural environments that

have inspired much of my work," she says. "I've welcomed the peacefulness of my new surroundings and the opportunity to set up a new, efficient work area in an airy, light-filled space."

Dotson continues to be fascinated with the potential of laminated vessels and she

I do brief sketches of ideas as they occur, or test new combinations of materials. When they coalesce into a more definite form, I start in.

has stripped recent vessels down to their basic structure. Dotson's environment continues to inspire her. "I am intrigued

Spiral Vessels, 2001. Italian poplar plywood, graphite; 9" high x 10¾" wide x 15½" deep. Just as a calligraphic brush stroke can contain an entire concept through gesture, Dotson uses form to capture experience and movement.

After Image, 2003. Baltic birch plywood; 7¾" high x 10¾" wide x 13½" deep. Says Dotson, "Animation and beauty may be found in the coexistence of opposites: positive and negative, light and dark, form and space."

Crosswinds, 1990. Wenge, maple; 6¼" high x 16¼" diameter; permanent collection, Los Angeles County Museum of Art.

by the features of the landscape and what they reveal about the past: traces of the sea that once covered the land, chronological arrangements of rock layers in many colors, changing compositions of light and shadow, and the cross-bedding lines left in sandstone by ancient winds. The layered patterns change over time as wind and water shape the surfaces. My laminated wood vessels are an expression of the landscape images. I shape the layered wood to reveal compositions of patterns that change as I work, and change again from the observer's perspective."

Dotson prepares a turning blank by gluing layers of plywood together. She visualizes how the turning is to look when done, and inserts wedge-shaped layers accordingly.

After roughing out the form on the band saw, Dotson is ready to mount the wood on the lathe.

The work takes shape on the lathe.

Removed from the lathe, Dotson saws into the work, then refines the edges.

Dotson applies tape to mask areas she does not want to dye, then she brushes on the concentrated aniline colors.

Sunlight Series #22, 2004. Curly birch and ebonized walnut, 9¼" high x 7¼" diameter. Dotson says the layers of wood echo the sedimentary rock landscapes of the Southwestern United States.

RON LAYPORT

Surface Work Will Not Cover Up Poor Form

Ron Layport interprets the natural world in the language employed by ancient cultures, but seen through the lens of contemporary art and design. Using animal effigies combined with vessel forms, he clarifies the connection between contemporary wood art and approaches employed by humankind for centuries. "I've always been

---

I approach it like a canvas. Even though I know what I am hoping to achieve, I try to be receptive to opportunities and changes of direction as they present themselves. The piece continues to evolve like a painting.

---

interested in work of the unknown artist," Layport says. "Work made a thousand years ago, that speaks of personal struggle, daily life, mystery, and ceremony."

When Layport designed and built furniture two decades ago, he worked like the itinerate builders of the 1800s whose designs were dictated by circumstance, tools, and materials. He found a degree of respectability in that, and it remains true of the work he creates today. The transition from creating one-of-a-kind furniture to turned vessels began when Layport wanted to learn to make round legs and feet. He was unaware of artistic woodturning. As a birthday present, his wife and children signed him up for a weekend workshop with a Pennsylvania woodturner who just happened to be the pioneering artist, David Ellsworth (page xi). The experience was a serendipitous introduction to the

All photos by Chuck Fuhrer

ABOVE

Residing in Pittsburgh and working in a basement studio, Layport often travels to experience vast natural spaces.

OPPOSITE

Incarnation of the Salmon King, 2006. Sycamore, ebony, brass, copper wire, pigment, dye; 14¼" high x 11" wide x 7" deep. *Incarnation of the Salmon King* is part of a series—Vessels from a Distant Dance—exploring the turned vessel form as a ceremonial or life mask. Layport uses wood and space to create a segmented effect. Stylized ebony fins support the object and create a sense of motion and mystery.

lathe and sounded the end of Layport's furniture career. He spent the weekend learning to turn a bowl and a hollow form, and never quite got to the table leg. He was immediately taken with the possibilities of a newly discovered art form.

Layport has been inspired by honesty to material and process. As the majority of his pieces address the natural world, it is not surprising he is driven by ecological considerations to prefer domestic woods that are found locally. "With few exceptions, I work with common hardwoods destined for fuel or landfill," Layport says. "I prefer local maple, cherry and, most of all, sycamore. If I hear chainsaws, meaning tree crews are working in the area, I get in the truck and go find them. Ideally, I prefer turning freshly cut green material, but more often have to get to it within the year."

Lathe Keeps Him Grounded

It is obvious Layport commits a great deal of time to his carving, yet he considers turning to be the basis of all of his work. "Though much of my work is 'post-turned,' the turned form must be valid before I proceed with sculpting. Surface work will not cover up poor form. Those turned vessels and bowls may sit around for months before they are further designed and worked, so they have to be pleasing as turned objects. I would have lost both focus and interest long ago, had it not been for the idea of working with the turned form. The lathe keeps me grounded, and brings structure and discipline to my work."

When he is turning wood, Layport may work for a week or ten days at a time. For vessels he uses the full diameter of a log, turning into end-grain, whereas for bowls he

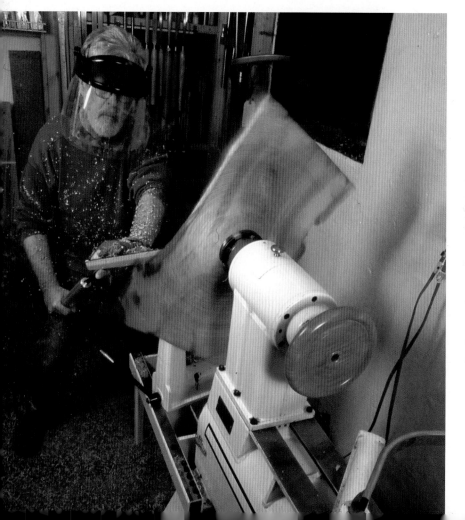

turns directly from the split log, untrimmed. "They are lethal—like propellers—because I am often turning as much as sixty percent air." Throughout the process, he remains open to unplanned "contributions" from the wood itself. For instance, flaws in the wood often become negative space in the final design—material to be cut away.

Once Layport knows what he wants to do with a piece, the sculpting and refining may take as many as five or six weeks at the bench, primarily using rotary tools. Yet, he doesn't depend upon modern technology to provide for all of his needs. "I use anything that addresses the problem at hand: broken saw blades with tape handles, bits made

My work is about leaving part of myself with the piece. It happens somewhere between the head, the hands and the heart.

of old safety pins, a multitude of sanding devices, and plenty of glue for stabilization."

Once he has carved the piece, Layport spends what he calls "an inordinate period of time" finishing. Unlike some artists, he does not have one set way of finishing the work and remains open to what the individual piece requires. "I approach it like a canvas. Even though I know what I am hoping to achieve, I try to be receptive to opportunities and changes of direction as they present themselves. The piece continues to evolve like a painting."

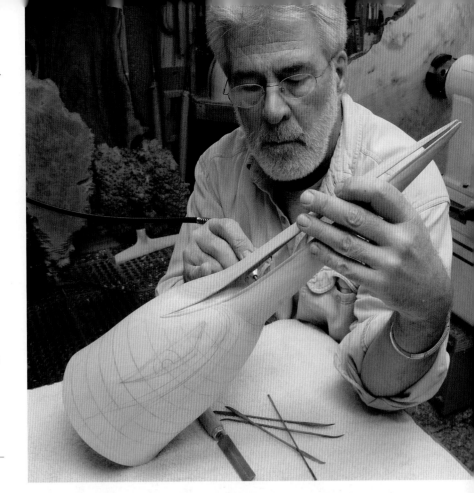

ABOVE TOP

Layport uses a combination of power tools and hand tools to carve and refine the sculpture. He says, "I use anything that addresses the problem at hand: broken saw blades with tape handles, bits made of old safety pins, a multitude of sanding devices, and plenty of glue for stabilization."

ABOVE BOTTOM

Layport spends what he calls "an inordinate period of time" finishing.

Wood is the Constant

Layport resides in Pittsburgh and works in a basement studio. "I long ago gave up the notion of having just the right setting to be creative. Romantic notions of a glass-walled workspace perched along the rim of the Great Lakes or the San Juan range have given way to a realization that is quite liberating. I am portable. I can travel to places that enrich me and inspire me to make things. My work space is for working." His experiences continue to inspire. "To come upon a wall of petroglyphs in a remote canyon is to sense the timelessness of the human condition and the continuum of art making. My work acknowledges my place in that continuum, rather than focusing on only the workspace, or the lathe, or the wood."

The creation of Layport's works of art is his means of connecting his past with his present, a means of finding his place in the natural world by making something of value using his hands. "Working with wood takes me back to my childhood in my dad's workshop. Even today, when I grab for one of his tools, I feel connected to the hand of my father. What he could do with a hand plane was nothing short of mesmerizing. I left my 40-year business career when computers began to eliminate the hands-on aspect of my work. 'Hands on' has become a rare privilege these days. I find that as I've become a better turner, I use fewer and fewer tools and am more at one with my work. My work is about leaving part of myself with the piece. It happens somewhere between the head, the hands and the heart."

Looking back at the initial weekend spent turning wood with David Ellsworth, Layport reflects that "a single exposure to the possibilities of turned wood objects changed the direction of my life. Wood is the constant that links one end of my life with the other."

Silk Morning, 2005. Maple, turned, sculpted, bleached, pigmented; 14½" high x 8½" diameter. "I wanted to achieve fluid motion and a sense of depth within the parameters of the vessel form. I sought rhythm and oneness, a continuum of elements, each flowing to the next. The mystery and wonder of an eco-system, perfected in the morning whiteness."

Spirit Whites (On Sky Blue Pale), 2006. Maple, turned, sculpted, bleached, pigmented; 10¼" high x 9" diameter. In creating *Spirit Whites*, Layport perfected the turned form, then reduced it to a nearly weightless object that defies, yet defines, the power of negative space. "To witness a gathering of spirits, on a blissful summer's afternoon, is to understand the mystical nature of this vessel," Layport says.

NEIL SCOBIE

Thinking of Running Water

Neil Scobie resides on the central east coast of Australia in a place called Bucca Creek, next to a state forest and close to pristine coastline famous for its beautiful beaches. In his ideal environment, Scobie built his own home using old bridge timbers to create soaring spaces filled with light from 20-foot high glass walls. Not far

I just get lost in thought looking into the bush. I even forget why I went out there, it's so quiet.

from the house is Scobie's enormous workshop with 2,400 square feet of space filled with every imaginable woodworking machine. The forest crowds right up to the workshop door and Scobie loves the peaceful atmosphere it brings. "Often I'll walk outside to get something and I just get lost in thought looking into the bush. I even forget why I went out there, it's so quiet."

Scobie was influenced from a young age by his grandfather, whom he describes as "a good amateur woodworker. He used to make boats and furniture, and even gunstocks. I still use his carving tools, which is important to me." Scobie originally trained as a teacher of woodwork, metalwork and industrial drawing. While he was a teacher, he developed his skills as a turner and, by the early '90s, it was an important sideline. He sold his work to a number of galleries and developed a national reputation as a quality turner. Eventually in 1990, after 20 years of teaching, he decided to concentrate on his own

Photo by Terry Martin

ABOVE

Scobie turns a rectangular slab of wood into a symmetrical blank with smoothly curving faces.

OPPOSITE

Erosion Forms, 2007. Australian blackwood; 7", 6", and 5" high. Grouping three forms together means they play off each other, enhancing the sense of captured energy.

Photo by Terry Martin

Photo by Terry Martin

woodwork. "I've never looked back," he proudly claims.

Scobie and his wife, Liz, now work from home, a remarkable partnership that spans a range of activities. Liz teaches textiles and produces her own line of textile art. Neil produces custom-made furniture and has recently been given a commission for the residence of the Australian Prime Minister. He also runs his own school and teaches woodcarving, furniture making, and turning. "I think it is very important to hand on the skills," he says.

The Evolution of Carved Bowls

Building on years of turning experience, Scobie also has created a line of work collected internationally. His carved bowls evolved from simpler functional vessels. At the start, he began the carving with a chain saw and then finished with traditional

---

People sometimes have to be told they were turned, as it looks unlikely.

---

carving tools. Now, he uses a number of different tools, including die grinders, power carving disks, flexible shaft tools, and many others. "I'll use whatever tool does the job most quickly," he says, "as long as it's safe." His workshop is a treasure trove of shop-made jigs and gadgets to make the work simpler and easier.

Scobie's best known pieces are his Erosion bowls. They are inspired by the patterns he sees around him in nature. "They remind me of the eroded gullies I saw when I was a boy on the farm. Also, I do a lot of white-water canoeing and I see patterns swirling in the water. When I make an Erosion piece, I'm thinking of running water and how it will wear a path through the earth." Scobie expanded the ideas from these bowls to

Photo by Terry Martin

make Erosion mirrors and then about seven years ago he began making wall sculptures, the largest up to five feet long. Now he also produces Erosion Forms in sets of three. In common with a lot of contemporary lathe work, it is not immediately obvious the pieces were turned, because the subsequent carving removes much of the evidence that they were ever on the lathe. Scobie explains: "People sometimes have to be told they were turned, as it looks unlikely."

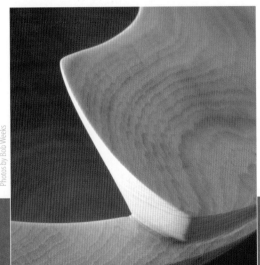

Photos by Rob Weeks

The Line of Least Resistance

It is significant that Scobie refers to the way water cuts through the landscape as it follows the line of least resistance. Scobie's work has that quality. When he teaches, Scobie always stresses the importance of working with the grain. This is, after all, following the line of least resistance. It gives his pieces a natural feel. They are not arbitrary shapes imposed on the wood. Like many well-known wood artists, Scobie is much imitated, but the copyists rarely achieve the same natural quality because they have not worked with the grain in the same fluid way.

It is this sense of rightness that distinguishes Scobie's work from pieces that try to impose clever shapes on wood regardless of its nature. Wood has distinct qualities that make working with the grain

BELOW
Nautilus Bowl, 2006. Huon pine; 9" x 3½". Scobie's Nautilus bowls are inspired by the swirling shapes of nautilus shells.

LEFT
Nautilus Bowl, detail.

Photo by Bob Weeks

of copying anyone else, so they're my own interpretation of the general idea. I saw the Swiss turner Sigi Angerer turning multi-axis, or inside-out fish, and I loved that, so I extended his technique to make my pods." Many of Scobie's pieces are painted by Liz, who has been enhancing his pieces for nearly twenty years. Her patterns also reflect what she sees in nature and their collaborations are among the most collectible pieces in the wood art field.

ABOVE

Nautilus Bowl, 2006. Collaboration with Liz Scobie. Australian red cedar, texture paste, acrylic paint; 6" x 2 ½". Liz Scobie has partly covered the wood with a finish reminiscent of mother-of-pearl.

RIGHT

After turning the faces, Scobie removes the chucking spigot from the center and rounds over the central portion to blend in with the body curves.

FAR RIGHT

Scobie sketches the shape to be carved onto the completed turning. He will remove the top portion, giving the impression the piece always was asymmetrical. He'll do most of the carving with powered tools, although details may be cut with traditional carving gouges.

Photo by Terry Martin

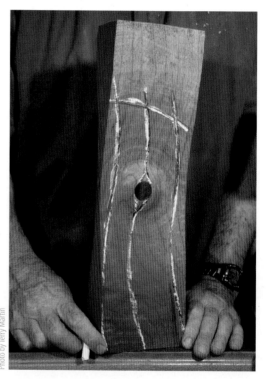
Photo by Terry Martin

both easier and visually more appealing. His Erosion series is not only a metaphor for nature, but a clear statement the old skills, learnt through hundreds of years of trial and error, still have a place in the creative world of wood art.

Scobie also produces a series he calls Pods. Scobie likes to acknowledge the influence of other turners and he explains the idea came from Mike Lee's pods (page 177). "I'd hate to ever be accused

Scobie is an energetic man who never seems to tire of life. His woodworking activities span almost the complete repertoire of craft and art and his endlessly positive outlook is enviable: "I love the variety of things we do here and I never get bored. I probably work too hard, but for me it's not work. I love it. I'm 54 now, but I still play volleyball, I go mountain-bike riding and I surf regularly." Who wouldn't enjoy such a life?

www.neilandlizscobie.com

Pods, 2007. Rosewood; largest 8½" x 3" x 1½". The pods have been carved after turning, and then partly stippled by burning.

Land and Sea Series, 2006. Collaboration with Liz Scobie. Australian red cedar, acrylic paint; 9⅜" x 1¼". *Land and Sea Series* is a fine example of the collaborative work between husband and wife. The land and seascapes of Australia inspire the patterns Liz paints.

MARK GARDNER

Drawn to the Rhythm of Repeated Carved Patterns

Mark Gardner started making furniture when he was sixteen and he acknowledges how important that was: "I believe the Shaker furniture I made when I was first learning to work with wood still influences me, particularly the simplicity of the Shaker aesthetic." His introduction to turning was through his father. "My

---

I will spend a few days or a week turning forms, then spend months altering, shaping, carving. and painting them.

---

father took a class from Al Stirt when I was in high school. I remember him coming home from the class with bags of bowls he had turned that week! It had a huge effect on me because furniture making is a slow process and the prospect of making something that quickly was attractive. I knew I wanted to turn bowls, but it wasn't until my class with John Jordan five years later I realized I could be good at it."

Gardner was inspired to try surface decoration after he saw the work of turner Clay Foster and furniture maker Kristina Madsen. The experience led him to study African and Oceanic artifacts in museums and books. "I'm drawn to the rhythm of repeated carved patterns on ceremonial and utilitarian objects," he explains. Now Gardner is among the group of turners who believe the lathe is only one tool among many. "Although I see the lathe as my primary tool and I still really enjoy the process of turning, most of the time spent working on

Photo by Nancy Barnett

ABOVE

Gardner and his son, Henry, walk the railway tracks near his home in the forested mountains of North Carolina.

OPPOSITE

Untitled, 2006. Walnut, paint; 43" x 19" x 5". In his recent work, Gardner has almost abandoned the lathe, even as the vestigial circular grooves betray the origins of this piece.

a piece occurs after the turning. I will spend a few days or a week turning forms, then spend months altering, shaping, carving, and painting them. I work from sketches as well as designing directly on the lathe. The latter is much more immediate and satisfying, but I find drawing to be a useful way of recording ideas when I'm unable to be in the studio."

Gardner shapes a log with his chainsaw, working with the grain, to create a larger piece than a turner might normally cut from a log of this size. "A piece of wood, its size and proportions, may suggest a particular approach to me," he says.

Gardner turns a big piece of wood on his enormous Oliver lathe, originally a patternmaker's machine. Such a heavy lathe is a real advantage when making large sculptural pieces.

A Garage Shop in the Appalachian Forest

Mark Gardner resides in the Appalachian mountains of western North Carolina, in a town of 650 residents called Saluda. It is an inspiring place for a woodworker to live because it is surrounded by trees, many of them quite old and large. Gardner's house nestles in a hollow between two hills and it has quite a lush feeling to it, so much so that in the autumn, when the leaves fall, Gardner looks forward to the broad sky of the winter landscape. He works in his garage where he has about 300 square feet packed with woodworking equipment, wood, and pieces in progress. In warm weather, he likes to open the garage door and work beneath the Japanese maples and cherry trees.

When Gardner started turning, he used green wood because it was easily available. "Practically speaking," he says, "I like that it is so easy to come by where I live." As his work has become more sculptural, he has used more seasoned wood, which brings its own problems. "Dry, stable material is hard to come by in large dimensions. I think this influences the work, as not every piece I want to make could come out of any random piece of wood. So, in a way, working with the wood the way I do, is a bit like using found objects in sculpture. I like that the material differs from species to species, and tree to tree, which presents new challenges and opportunities. I may have an idea for a piece and have to let it sit in a sketch book until the right piece of wood appears. In other cases, a piece of wood, its size and proportions, may suggest a particular approach to me and send me off in a whole

new direction. An example of this is the 'boat forms' that I make. I made the first few of these when I was trying to use some really nice but relatively small dogwood logs. They were only about six or seven inches in diameter, but about 24 inches long. I wanted to use the natural beauty of the material as well as give myself some surfaces to embellish. Without a specific piece in mind I turned long pod forms that were quartered lengthwise. This led me to further shape and embellish them to create the boat shape."

An Evolving Formality

Early in his career, Gardner made the decision to create a sense of formality with his vessels. He achieved formality by cutting away a turned rim with the bandsaw to create a pair of handles, as with *African Blackwood Bowl*. It is a simple but effective device, although it does require fine control on the band saw. Another effective touch is cutting bevels on the ends of the handles, giving the whole a more finely worked finish. While Gardner was clearly distancing his

ABOVE LEFT

With fine cuts from the gouge, Gardner creates the flattened top edge of a Boat Form—initially turned as a long pod shape, then sawn lengthwise into quarters.

ABOVE RIGHT

Maple Boxes, 1996. Bleached maple; 3" x 2" diameter. Gardner's early work included conventional lidded boxes like this little pair.

LEFT

African Blackwood Bowl, 2000. African blackwood; 3" x 3" x 4". *African Blackwood Bowl*, a handled bowl with a delicately sawn strip that connects the handles, is a fine example of Gardner's early work.

Tea Set, 2000. Ebonized ash; 7" x 3" x 11". Working with a large piece of wood, Gardner turns the vessel in the center of a wide disk of wood. Then, he saws most of the disk away, leaving just enough for the handles.

Offering Bowl, 2004. Maple, paint; 4" x 32" x 12". The circular lines clearly show *Offering Bowl* was turned on the lathe. It appears the dovetails and raised portions were in the wood when it was turned, but it is a fine illusion because Gardner added them afterward.

pieces from simple functional vessels, there was often a fleeting reference to function, even though his pieces generally aren't meant to be used. In a sense, he is paying respect to earlier cultures. A good example is *Tea Set*, made in 2000. With their formal, winged extensions, it is not hard to see the link with a Japanese tea ceremony set. Gardner's work soon came to be a clear statement of non-function, even when its roots were clearly based on turned bowls. *Square Bowl* says: "I am to be looked at, perhaps handled, but not used!" If anything distinguishes his work, it

is this formality—a kind of serene simplicity that allows Gardner's pieces to work well when displayed in a ceremonial setting. They are among the best of the new works representing the adventurous innovation that has overtaken the field in recent years.

Gardner is now firmly among those who create sculpture on the lathe and he has developed a signature style, while his work continues to evolve. Most importantly, at 35, he is among the younger artists in the field, so we can look forward to many years of fine work to come.

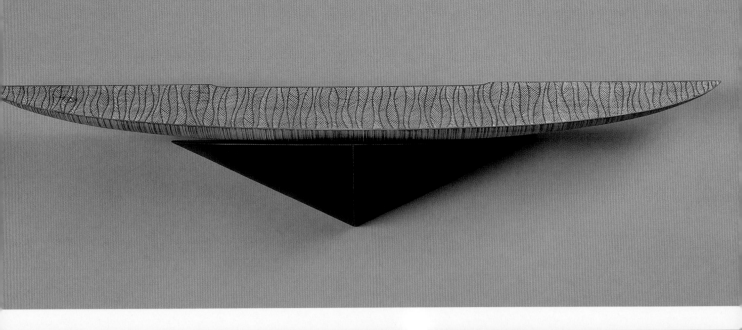

ABOVE TOP

Boat Form, 2006. Cherry, paint; 7" x 34" x 4". Mounted on its own wall stand, it is not immediately obvious that *Boat Form* was turned at all. However, the incised grooves on the underside were unmistakably made on the lathe.

ABOVE BOTTOM

Square Bowl, 2004. Walnut, milk paint; 2½" x 6" x 6". Gardner enjoys the contradiction of producing a square form on the lathe. He turns the top grooves on the spinning block, extending them into space where the wood ends. He enhances the visual contradiction by picking up the turned grooves in the top surface and flowing them over square edges.

RIGHT

Untitled Vessel, 2002. Ebonized maple; 8" x 5" diameter. The incised carving was inspired by Gardner's study of African and Oceanic artifacts in museums and books. He says he is "drawn to the rhythm of repeated carved patterns on ceremonial and utilitarian objects."

MARILYN CAMPBELL

Pushing the Designs While Keeping Them Simple

Marilyn Campbell didn't set out to be a woodturner. "I graduated from university with a degree in anthropology and expected just to get a job somewhere," Campbell says. "But, after graduation, my future husband and I decided we were going to build a boat and live a life of adventure sailing around the world. Turns out, I was

I began using epoxy when I wanted to achieve certain effects but didn't know how to do it. A little liquid wood solved the problems, and I just kept on using it.

more interested in the building than the sailing." Boat building introduced Campbell to both wood and epoxy and by the time their 36-foot sailboat was launched, she knew she wanted to continue working in wood. It was no small decision, because she was well aware that she knew very little about woodworking methods. She taught herself to turn from a book and found working on the lathe offered numerous creative possibilities, within the limits imposed by the machine. "I began using epoxy when I wanted to achieve certain effects but didn't know how to do it the proper way. A little liquid wood solved the problems I was having," she recalls. "I just kept on using it."

Campbell's highly original combination of wood and epoxy, both as a binding agent and a sculptural medium, allows her to create unique vessels that defy the limits of the traditional wooden form. She so artfully combines

All photos by Stephen Simeon

ABOVE

Campbell works in a small but efficient studio.

OPPOSITE

Full Regalia, 2006, holly, epoxy, cherry, purpleheart, paint; 9¾" high x 9½" long x 3" wide. Campbell says, "*Full Regalia*, being very formal and somewhat austere, echoes the pomp and pageantry of a royal parade."

Come Here Often?
2007, holly, epoxy,
paint, curly maple,
purpleheart, dye;
9" high x 7¾" long
x 2½" wide. Campbell
says, "*Come Here Often?*
brings to mind a
slightly inebriated gent
in formal attire trying
that age-old line."

her materials that it is not always easy to tell what is wood and what is plastic, nor is it easy to detect the lathe's circular argument in the final form. "I see the vessels as representing those grand social events set back in an era when elegance and style were the cultural ideal. I want the viewer to think of fine dinner parties, tuxes and tails, top hats and formal gowns,

and I have chosen titles to reflect these scenarios," Campbell says.

The first person to have a significant influence on Campbell's work was Stephen Hogbin (page x), who she first met more than two decades ago. She only had been turning wood for a few years and was making small functional works for craft fairs. "I didn't really know what I was doing,"

Persuasion, 2006,
holly, epoxy, cherry,
purpleheart, epoxy,
fiberglass, paint;
7⅝" high x 8" long
x 2½" wide.

Campbell recalls. "He showed me turning could be art. It completely turned my head around and changed my view of what I was making and why." Many years later, Binh Pho (page 163) also influenced her work. "I admire certain qualities in his work and I

Wood has a warm personality lacking in other materials. It's so versatile—the variety seems endless and its character can change depending on the wood. I can manipulate wood in a way I find very satisfying.

---

wanted those same qualities for my own," she says, noting Pho's creations have a "cultured look, delicacy and elegance."

Campbell's works are both fragile and complex. While she works, she is always aware that "at any stage I can, by some small, careless move, erase hours of work already invested in the piece. Because I'm a low-tech person, I have so far solved all the challenges with simple solutions and just plain mindful care. Not that that's any guarantee." And, like many of today's leading artists, for Campbell the lathe is merely the starting place. She does much, and often most, of the work after the piece comes off the lathe. She says, "Because there are so many small steps in the making of one piece and each piece takes weeks to complete, I am always trying to improve my methods to make the process faster and more efficient."

Because of the materials she works with, the technical challenges Campbell faces are not the usual ones with which other woodturners deal. "My problems

are things such as working out the best way to get cling wrap to lay into convex contours for molding purposes, or building enough strength into some of the resin components," she said. Even so, her real creative challenges are centered on design: "I am trying to push the designs to finer levels while still keeping them varied and simple."

Celebration, 2006, holly, epoxy, cherry, purpleheart, paint; 8½" high x 8½" long x 2¾" wide. "In keeping with my theme of high-society decadence, I wanted to give this piece a mood of music and motion," Campbell says. "A celebration of life's good times."

While Campbell plans on experimenting with other materials, thus far wood remains central to her work. "Although I can appreciate other mediums for their own unique qualities, I find wood has a warm personality lacking in other materials," she said. "It's so versatile—the variety seems endless and its character can change depending on the wood, as well as on what treatments and enhancements I use. I can manipulate wood in a way I find very satisfying. I have to say a big part of its appeal has to do with its reputation in my mind as a serious medium and the exclusive realm of master craftsmen whose skill

ABOVE

Campbell's hometown of Kincardine, Ontario, is shaped by Lake Huron, visible in the distance as an early winter storm rolls in across Harbour Beach.

RIGHT

Overlooking the harbor, the Kincardine lighthouse and museum is the focal point of the town's marine heritage.

had been hard won after years of intense apprenticeship. That's certainly no group of which I ever could be a part." Although she does much of the work off the lathe, the turning process remains essential. "It defines what I can and cannot make, and gives me limits so I don't feel lost in too much choice. But, however essential, it is still only one step of many used in completing a piece."

A Great Lakes Farm Town

Campbell lives and works in Kincardine, a small, friendly town on the edge of Lake Huron in southwestern Ontario, Canada. The Scottish origins of the town are still celebrated, with a pipe band parade every Saturday night in the summer months, with a good portion of the town marching along behind, and good-natured "fines" handed out to people caught not wearing their plaid on Fridays. It is a rural community, rooted in farming, yet today the nuclear power plant north of town is the largest single employer. Lake Huron gives Kincardine a picturesque beach and harbor that make it a popular summer

attraction. While the harbor was once used for commercial shipping on the Great Lakes, now it is mainly used for fishing and recreational boating. Campbell's husband, Jim, has been the lighthouse keeper there for 25 years.

The couple have kept the boat they built together there since its launching in 1976 and they spend several weeks each summer sailing around northern Lake Huron and Georgian Bay. Winters in Kincardine are long and the lake-effect snow is heavy, making winter travel treacherous. For Campbell, however, the season is a major attraction because she enjoys all of the cross-country skiing the area has to offer.

The natural world has been a constant inspiration for Campbell, but she has become increasingly interested in strong design principles and the exploration of flowing lines, contrast, and geometric elements. Her combinations of wide-ranging influences, which include the art deco stylings of vintage handbags, have resulted in boldly original sculptural works that expand the language of the medium.

www.marilyncampbell.ca

HOW CAMPBELL WORKS

Campbell's work requires careful planning and each piece must be designed on paper first. She starts with a blank of holly, a hard wood that is almost pure white. She first transfers the drawing onto the wood, then saws and discards the volumes that will be replaced with black epoxy. Then she arranges the remaining holly pieces to fit the paper design, and fills in the spaces with a thickened mixture of epoxy. When the epoxy has set, she can turn the outside of the blank. At this point the piece looks like a round cake pan with one flat side.

While the piece is still mounted on the lathe faceplate, Campbell takes it off the lathe and covers it tightly in plastic wrap. She mixes up more thickened epoxy and spreads it over the plastic wrap, using the turning as a mold. Once the epoxy has set, the assemblage goes back on the lathe so she can turn the epoxy down to a thin shell, to form the overlay. Now she can pop the epoxy skin off the wood, and cut it to shape according to her design. Then she paints it black, and lays it over the holly so the white wood shows through the pierced openings.

After making the skin, Campbell turns the inside of the vessel, saws it in half, and joins the two parts along their rim to form the sides of the vessel. She makes a wooden spine to join the vessel halves together, usually painting it black to match the epoxy. Only after the two halves have been textured, pierced, and painted, and the overlay has been shaped, textured, pierced, and painted, and the spine has been turned and painted, is she at last ready to assemble the finished vessel. She carefully glues it all together.

To make the overlay, Campbell uses the turning itself as a mold, spreading on an epoxy mixture, which, when cured, she will turn down to a thin skin.

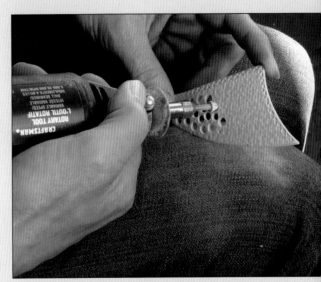

After turning, Campbell removes the thin skin from the mold and cuts, shapes, textures and pierces it to create the overlay components.

After painting the overlay, Campbell very carefully glues it to one face of the vessel.

STEVEN KENNARD

Technique Is Important, But Secondary to Getting There

Steven Kennard is inspired by textures he sees in the natural world and his surface texturing techniques have developed from a need to create visual and tactile illusions. An important influence on his forms and textures are the years he spent creating illusions for

I am a great believer in feeling my way through the things I make, not measuring, or at least keeping measurements to a bare minimum. If it feels good and pleases my eye, then it is successful for me.

theatrical performances. During that time he learned to create and/or accentuate impressions of size and shape. "The experience still serves me in the way I carve and texture my pieces," Kennard says. "I constantly experiment and try out ideas before incorporating them into the finished pieces."

Kennard's small sculptural boxes combine woodturning, carving, and the creation of various surface textures. Kennard's interest in lidded forms lies in the mystery of a closed container. "Perhaps it's a progression from the infinite number of containers that surround our lives. Our homes and much of what they hold are, in one way or another, containers. We even make our departure in one!"

The wood he uses also inspires Kennard. "I love the sensuality of wood—to the touch and to the eye. It's such a warm material with a natural beauty and

All photos courtesy the artist

ABOVE

Kennard band saws the blank for a lidded box from a richly figured block of burl wood.

OPPOSITE

Lost Orchard, 2007. African blackwood, cocobolo, thuya, ivory; 2½" high x 3⅛" diameter. *Lost Orchard* was inspired by the old apple orchards in the Annapolis Valley, Nova Scotia, where the artist lives: "Their stark appearance against the winter landscape will be sadly mourned as these are being decimated around us."

Kennard resides in the Annapolis Valley of Nova Scotia.

different inherent qualities in each of the species, giving me a huge choice for different applications and decorative effects."

Kennard's career as a woodturner began when he made custom furniture and restored antiques in Suffolk, England, in the 1970s. "The turning started off as components for furniture—mostly spindle work—such as legs for tables and chairs," he recalls. "My first deviations were my early bowls and boxes. They had a very traditional look to them, taking elements from the furniture with which I had been working."

Soon after immersing himself in the craft, Kennard saw the potential for self-expression and began developing his distinctive style of work. "There have been very few direct influences on my work. When I started turning, there were few artists working with a lathe and the work being done was not documented as it is now," says Kennard, who worked in isolation for years. Eventually, he stumbled across Stephen Hogbin's book *Woodturning,*

The Purpose of the Object. "It really opened a door, as the idea was so new to me—the idea something that primarily turns round objects could be used as a starting point to produce sculptural pieces that left you

---

I find listening to music inspires me and aids my concentration. I have an eclectic taste in music and it can set a mood for the whole work experience.

---

wondering how they were created. Hogbin's works (page x) were worlds away from the things generally produced on a lathe at that time. Seeing the lathe as just a part of the process was a revelation to me."

Kennard also credits David Pye's approach to his craft as an influence. "I frequently compare (what David Pye called) the 'workmanship of certainty' to the 'workmanship of risk.' The latter is the way we must follow if we are ever to develop as creators of beautiful objects."

From France to an Old Farm in Nova Scotia

In 1989, Kennard moved to France to reside in a 400-year-old farmhouse where he continued his artistic turning and furniture making. He still was producing bowls, but they were now very thin-walled, wet-turned forms. He created candlesticks and lamp bases in a semi-traditional style, but they were an early start to his interest in surface decoration, as he used watercolor paints on them. At the same time, Kennard's boxes began to take on personalities of their own and eventually became his most compelling work.

"My time in France saw a gradual departure from the safe styles of tradition," says Kennard of this period of experimentation and exploration. "It was a time that led to where my work is today." Kennard found his first success as a woodturner there and was invited to exhibit his work in various galleries and exhibitions in the South of France. In the early 1990s, he was chosen to be one of the "38 Artisans of the Aquintaine," exhibiting in the beautiful old cloisters in the famous wine town of Saint Emilion, and was one of three chosen to represent artist-craftsmen of the area for an exhibition in Fukuoka, Japan.

In 1997, Kennard moved to Nova Scotia on the East Coast of Canada, where he still resides and works on an old farm property in the beautiful Annapolis Valley. His workshop is in an old converted barn surrounded by landscaped gardens that provide an ideal place to sit in the warm sun and enjoy a cup of tea. A member of the local arts and crafts community, he is a juried member of the Nova Scotia Designer Crafts Council and also on its standards committee.

Confidently Self-Taught

The confidence Kennard has gained over the years enables him to follow his ideas wherever they lead and he has furthered this exploration through each successive piece. "Removing the boundaries and restrictions I felt in these earlier years has been a release, artistically speaking," he says. He is entirely self-taught and has developed his own technical approaches to achieve the effects

The shavings fly as Kennard hollows the body of a little wooden box in the same series as *Lost Orchard*.

Kennard's house, workshop/studio (red building) and gallery fill the old farm buildings.

he is looking for. "I am not preoccupied with what is the 'right way' or 'wrong way' to do something, providing I can achieve what I want. My focus is on the final work."

Kennard's works are usually planned totally in his mind, with the occasional sketch to serve as a reminder. While the lathe was once used from the start to finish of the piece, today Kennard views it as the "jumping-off point" for his sculptural boxes. Kennard's lathe work may account for 50 to 75 percent of the total time spent creating a piece. Technical challenges arise because of the precise nature of his work, and because of scale limitations due to materials. He favors African blackwood because it is stable and ideal for creating the forms and textures he envisions, but it does not come in large pieces.

Kennard uses a General 260 lathe and a small selection of high-speed steel turning tools he frequently re-shapes to accommodate the current project. For texturing, he employs a flexible-shaft tool with a variety of burrs, using an optical visor to view the fine detailing. "Technique is important, but secondary to getting there," he says. "I am a great believer in feeling my way through the things I make, not measuring, or at least keeping measurements to a bare minimum. If it feels good and pleases my eye, then it is successful for me."

A less obvious, yet tremendously important, influence on his work is music, which can be heard wafting out of his studio throughout the day. "I find listening to music inspires me and aids my concentration. I have an eclectic taste in music and it can set a mood for the whole work experience."

www.stevenkennard.com

LOUISE HIBBERT

The Lathe Gives My Work Rhythm and Balance

Louise Hibbert was born and raised near Southampton on the south coast of England. She completed an art degree in 1994 and during the next few years developed various production lines of pens and kitchenware. After moving to North Wales in 1996, she became friends with Hayley Smith, page 7, who impressed Hibbert with her "approach to her work, her integrity, and meticulous attention to detail." Hibbert's own style developed quite quickly. "My inspiration evolved from my fascination with the natural world, particularly marine life, microscopic creatures, plants, and fossils that together offer a fantastic repertoire of imagery," she says. "Through exploration, I discovered the work of the nineteenth century biologist and illustrator Ernst Haeckel, whose sumptuous illustrations are constantly echoed in my work." Hibbert was drawn particularly to Haeckel's studies of radiolarians. The single-celled microorganisms have a mesmerizing and delicate beauty that inspired Haeckel and enriched the Art Nouveau movement. After visiting the United States in 2001, Hibbert married American Doug Finkel, a fellow wood artist, and in 2004, they moved to Virginia.

Photos courtesy the artist unless otherwise indicated

ABOVE

Hibbert develops a design in her studio.

LEFT

Louise Hibbert, her husband, Doug Finkel, and their dog, Bella, reside in an Airstream trailer on their property in rural Virginia, while building their house and workshops.

OPPOSITE

Radiolarian Vessel VII, 2004. English sycamore, silver, texture paste, acrylic inks; 6" wide. "*Radiolarian Vessel VII* evolved from an electron microscope image of a radiolarian, a type of zooplankton found throughout the oceans," Hibbert says. "Through the series they started to take on some crab-like characteristics."

Collaboration with a Jeweler

In 2001, Louise Hibbert began collaborating with jeweler, Sarah Parker-Eaton. She believes the experience has pushed her work to new levels, greatly expanded its possibilities, and led to new and exciting experiences. "I feel fantastically lucky to have found and collaborated with a maker whose work I admire and whose style, inspiration, and working process are so close to my own. She also has become a great friend." Recently, the two worked together on Genus Australis, a collaborative project inspired by the Western Australian landscape, following a month's residency in Perth, Australia, in 2003. It was created as part of a larger mission to draw attention to the value of Western Australia's unique natural resources and the critical importance of conservation and ecological sustainability. "I wanted to reflect the distinctive beauty of Western Australia's indigenous flora. I wanted to capture the forms, patterns, textures, and colors honed to perfection through millions of years of evolution. The pieces are made to be picked up, explored, and enjoyed."

"Each day is different," Hibbert offers when asked about her creative process. "If I am working on a project with Sarah, we will start by spending a week or so together talking, looking at books and objects, possibly going on field trips, drawing, and

BELOW

Rumex, collaboration with Sarah Parker-Eaton, 2004. English sycamore, silver, texture paste, acrylic inks; 4½" wide. Part of the Genus Australis series, this dark, textured fruit capsule, with its hooked teeth, opens to reveal a vibrantly colored treasure within.

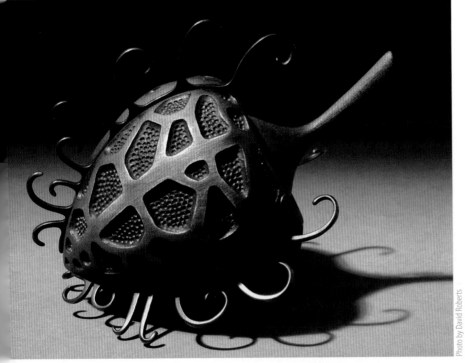

Photo by David Roberts

RIGHT TOP

Corymbia, collaboration with Sarah Parker-Eaton, 2004. Maple, silver, gold, acrylic inks. 5" wide. "The barrel-shaped woody pods of the *Corymbia ficifolia*, or red flowering gum, inspired Corymbia," Hibbert says. "For me, the magnificent gum trees are an icon of the Australian landscape."

RIGHT BOTTOM

Dicoryne Box, collaboration with Sarah Parker-Eaton, 2005. English sycamore, western Australian myall, silver, gold texture paste, acrylic inks; 6½" long. "*Dicroryne conferta*, the main inspiration behind this box, is a hydroid—part of a group of exquisite marine animals," Hibbert explains. "The silver spines on its edges represent the cilia that propel it through the sea." The small scale of the piece encourages handling and the spines require the same careful handling as the small creature might. The magnets holding the box together give Dicoryne Box a little extra life when the box snaps closed.

Photo by David Roberts

Photo by Louise Hibbert

drinking lots of tea. It is the part of my work I enjoy most and when I feel most creative. Anything can happen." The careful planning of each piece on paper is vital. "The drawings I create for every piece are to scale, often with a side and top view. Sarah's drawings will be covered in notes about the metal parts—lengths of posts needed, oxidization—while mine have details about the wood species, colors, textures, and dimensions. Our collaborative approach ensures two distinct materials merge into one fluid form."

The two then work separately. "If Sarah starts a piece it is always a thrilling moment to open the parcel and see what she has made. Often it surpasses what I am expecting and inspires me to greater heights. I will work on a piece continuously until it is done, generally starting at my Wadkin Bursgreen BZL lathe, an old friend I brought with me from the United Kingdom."

The Genus Australis project offered a number of invigorating challenges involving new, difficult forms and the need for a very different look to the wood's surface. "Previous surfaces I'd created had been reflective and glowing, inspired by vivid, sleek marine creatures, evolved to glide through their oceanic environment. The new pieces had to reflect the earthy weathered seedpods, roughened by the harsh Australian climate. I moved away from the smooth polyester resin and used a granular texture paste. I also started scorching and scratching the wood's surface. Some of the turning and carving pushed me to my limits, but when I felt a piece was successful, I'd feel a great sense of achievement."

Photo by David Roberts

An Expansive Use of Materials

Although Hibbert is known for her use of paint and polyester resin, her collaborations with Parker-Eaton have allowed for a more expansive use of materials. However, wood remains her medium of choice and the lathe is still the best means of creating her forms. "When I began to work in wood, it was not because I was attracted to straight lines and joinery. I chose wood because I can shape it into forms with flowing lines or crisp details. Having been alive, wood has a warmth that resonates with my designs. It is important to me that people are able to sense this quality when they interact with my pieces. Many of my designs evolve from shapes with organic symmetry and the technique allows me to create these forms quickly. I find that using the lathe gives my work rhythm and balance, almost like a structural backbone within each piece. As human beings, we are drawn to patterns and symmetrical forms. In nature, recognition means survival, symmetry equates to health and beauty."

When Hibbert married fellow woodworker Doug Finkel and moved to the United States, the two set out to find a

Thomasia, collaboration with Sarah Parker-Eaton, 2004. English sycamore, silver, gold, texture paste, acrylic inks; 6" high. The ovary of *Thomasia foliosa*, with an outer surface covered with short, dense, star-like hairs, inspired *Thomasia*. The *Thomasia foliosa* woodland shrub grows in Western Australia.

home in Gloucester, Virginia. "We looked at a number of properties, but found nothing that came close to meeting our needs, aesthetically or in practical terms, so we felt building a home was the only way we would get the character and integrity we wanted," Hibbert says. The two felt lucky to find a beautiful, undulating seven-acre patch of deciduous woodland and began building an Appalachian Cape Cod log house. "I

I wanted to capture the forms, patterns, textures, and colors honed to perfection through millions of years of evolution. The pieces are made to be picked up, explored, and enjoyed.

think this is a beautiful American style," she says. "Traditional, but sophisticated and enduring. It has been wonderful moving to the land and enjoying the birds, wildlife, and woodland that slopes gently away from the house toward the streams." Hibbert often spends an afternoon walking their dog, Loki, around the Beaverdam Reservoir, which boasts snapping turtles, ospreys, herons, and even the occasional bald eagle. The experiences are important for Hibbert. "It is not just the beauty of its surface that attracts me to nature, it is the harmonious order of its parts, the science, the way it continuously finds solutions to problems. It is both awe-inspiring and fascinating. Through my work, I hope to bring this wonder and appreciation of nature to a wider audience."

Heuchera Box, 2007. English sycamore, copper, texture paste, acrylic inks; 3½" long. *Heuchera Box* incorporates the range of techniques Hibbert uses in her work, including carving, airbrushing, resin spines, pyrography, metalwork and hidden magnets.

Peplus Box, 2007. English sycamore, silver, acrylic inks; 3" long. "I love the undulating surface of the English euphorbia seed that inspired *Peplus Box*," Hibbert says. "Its size allows it to fit snugly in your hand when closed."

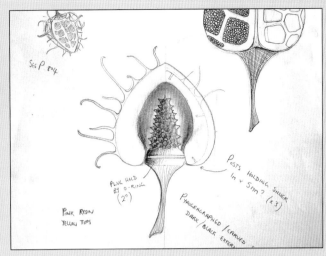

Hibbert makes careful drawings of the plant and animal forms that inspire her.

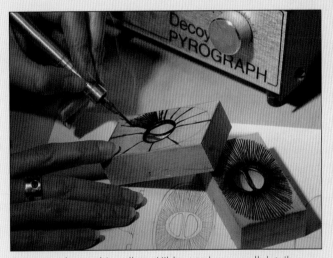

She uses a jeweler's saw to cut tiny wood and metal inlays.

A pyrography machine allows Hibbert to burn small details into the wood.

With texture paste and a steady hand, Hibbert makes a raised pattern of dots on the wood, a process she calls "blobbing."

Hibbert sprays color onto her work using a tiny airbrush with acrylic paints and concentrated dyes.

THIERRY MARTENON

It's Good to Work with Almost Nothing

In a field where innovation is highly valued, Thierry Martenon is perhaps the most innovative of all. He has a genius for producing the unexpected and in a remarkably short time, he has established himself as one of the most collectible artists in the field. Martenon explains how he came to be a wood artist: "I reside in the

---

I live in a small village where everybody knows everybody. It is a long way to the modern life in the city and we live like people did 60 years ago. I need that to create my pieces. I need to be quiet.

---

mountains where the only raw materials are wood and stone. Everything is made of wood—houses, tools, roofs, everything. If you are not a farmer, you are a carpenter, a cabinetmaker, a logger, or a sawyer. My grandfather was a sawyer and my other grandfather carted wood with horses. In my village, there was an old woodturner, and when I was young, I was fascinated by him. He was like a magician. Later, I saw the work of Jean-Francois Escoulen on show and he was the second magician in my life. I had no choice, I wanted to become a magician."

Martenon is an unpretentious man who is visibly embarrassed, and pleased, when his work is praised. His humility probably has much to do with where he was born and still resides. "I live in the south-east of France in the Alps where the countryside is beautiful. In the mountains, we have long winters, which are good for working. I was born here and I love to live here. I live

Photo by Audrey Martenon. Other photos courtesy the artist unless otherwise indicated.

ABOVE
Martenon burns his signature into the wood with a pyrograph.

OPPOSITE
Untitled #14022004, 2004. Walnut, elm, veneer, slate; 36" high x 6" diameter. Patches of veneer give a remarkable textured effect to the surface of this turned form.

in a small village where everybody knows everybody and the young people help the oldest. It is a long way to the modern life in the city and we live as people did 60 years ago. I need that to create my pieces. I need to be quiet." It certainly is that. Behind his

---

When I get a good idea, I run to the stock of wood and it starts. It's like wild dance and until it is complete, all my brain can think about is that idea.

Martenon has built his workshop into a restored barn in his home village of Le Désert in the French Alps.

Photo by Audrey Martenon

home, sheep graze in the fields that sweep up to the looming escarpment of the forested plateau that dominates the landscape. In a hectic world where many of us dream of such peace, he is a lucky man to be so comfortable in his identity and sense of place.

In his peaceful environment, Martenon can work without interruption, surging into activity when an idea strikes. "First of all, I take my sketch book and, sitting in my comfortable old chair, I draw. It could take days and days. When I get a good idea, I run to the stock of wood and it starts. It's like wild dance and until it is complete, all my brain can think about is that idea."

Martenon's approach is an amazing change for someone who had a traditional French training as a cabinetmaker. After secondary school, Martenon attended the Greta Tête d'Or institute in Lyon and graduated in 1990, as a cabinetmaker. He worked at that until 1998, when he decided to devote himself to turning. During this time, he also was fascinated with graphic arts and continued to learn all he could. It was not long before he left behind traditional turning and allowed his artistic instincts to take over.

Serenity in Simple Forms

Martenon uses simple forms, aiming for a degree of serenity. Martenon's surface treatments give his pieces such extraordinary qualities. The treatments seem simple, but they are the result of meticulous work. Even seemingly brutal tools like the chainsaw, acid, or a blowtorch are wielded with great care. Martenon explains, "I like to create a contrast between light and shadow. The notches in the wood create the downstrokes and upstrokes that play with light. Polishing creates effects of darkness and light as well. The wood also adds its own qualities. I mainly use local woods such as walnut, maple, and ash. By combining different materials, such as copper, stone, linen, tin, or resin with the wood, I can give each piece its own character." The treatments are completely unlike the work of anybody else in the field. The strips of veneer look like metal hammered onto the surface of the wood. Thin sections of slate laid edge-on to fill the tops of vessels create a startling contrast and the slate has a harsh tactile quality that contrasts deeply with the feel of wood. The sculptural pieces have clearly been influenced by Martenon's interest in graphic art and they often look like sketches solidified, drawn concepts brought to three-dimensional fruition.

Working from a restored barn in his village, Martenon is determined to keep his processes simple and he is not obsessed with equipment. "It's good to work with almost nothing. I tinker and invent. I've made textures simply by rubbing a handful of gravel on the wood. You can waste a lot of time freeing yourself from technique. To be honest, for me the lathe is just a tool like any other tool. But, it has given me the taste of simple shapes, pure design. It has been an important part of my artistic life."

In 2004, Martenon stopped naming his pieces. Now he gives them a simple number for identification. Possibly Martenon believed the search for original names was distracting from the simplicity of his forms. The response would be in keeping with the

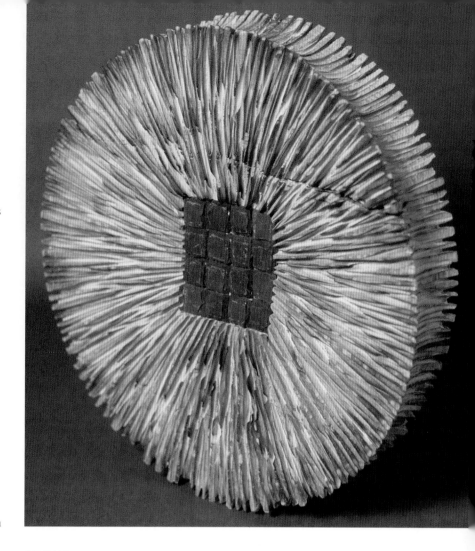

ABOVE

Untitled #06012005, 2005. Maple, slate; 19" diameter. Martenon's juxtaposition of two unlikely materials, slate and wood, is typical of his approach. He is unrestricted by conventional expectations.

BELOW

Untitled #05052004, 2004. Walnut and slate; 22" long x 6" diameter. *Untitled #05052004* resembles a ceremonial vessel to be held in both hands. The carving on the body reflects the edges of the embedded slate.

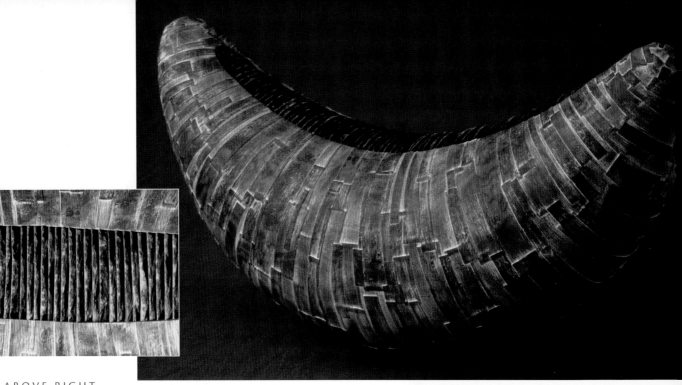

ABOVE RIGHT

Untitled #27022004, 2004. Walnut, veneer, slate; 16" long x 6" wide x 9" high. *Untitled #27022004*, a horned vessel, embodies all the elements of Martenon's work—an unexpected shape, juxtaposed materials, and superb surface treatment.

ABOVE INSET

Untitled #27022004. Detail. Cutting slate with this degree of precision takes a lot of skill.

old dictum he follows—less is more. It also challenges viewers to interpret his work as they will.

During recent years, French wood artists have explored texture and surface treatment perhaps more than any other artists in the field, and Martenon has done it more

---

It's good to work with almost nothing. I tinker and invent. I've made textures simply by rubbing a handful of gravel on the wood.

---

than any of them—with total mastery. Martenon's work develops so rapidly it is difficult to follow his progress. While he moves on the rest of us can only watch, admire, and dream of keeping up.

Untitled #21122001, 2001. Maple and white acrylic; 16" high x 8¾" diameter. *Untitled #21122001* is an example of Martenon's earlier vessels. Wonderfully proportioned and simply decorated, the form is perfect.

www.thierrymartenon.com

Photos by Audrey Martenon

To show the creation of art can be a simple process, Martenon turns a simple disk on the lathe.

After sanding the disk, Martenon cuts a square and smooth hole in its center using conventional carving tools.

Martenon chars the surface with an oxy-acetylene torch. Done quickly, the charring is only superficial and does not crack the wood.

Outside Martenon uses a wire brush to remove the loose carbon from the wood surface.

Martenon bevels the edges of the piece using a rasp, then sands it and applies an oil finish.

The finished piece: the beveled edges highlight the simple form, contrasting with the burnt surface and its exaggerated grain. Art does not always have to be complicated.

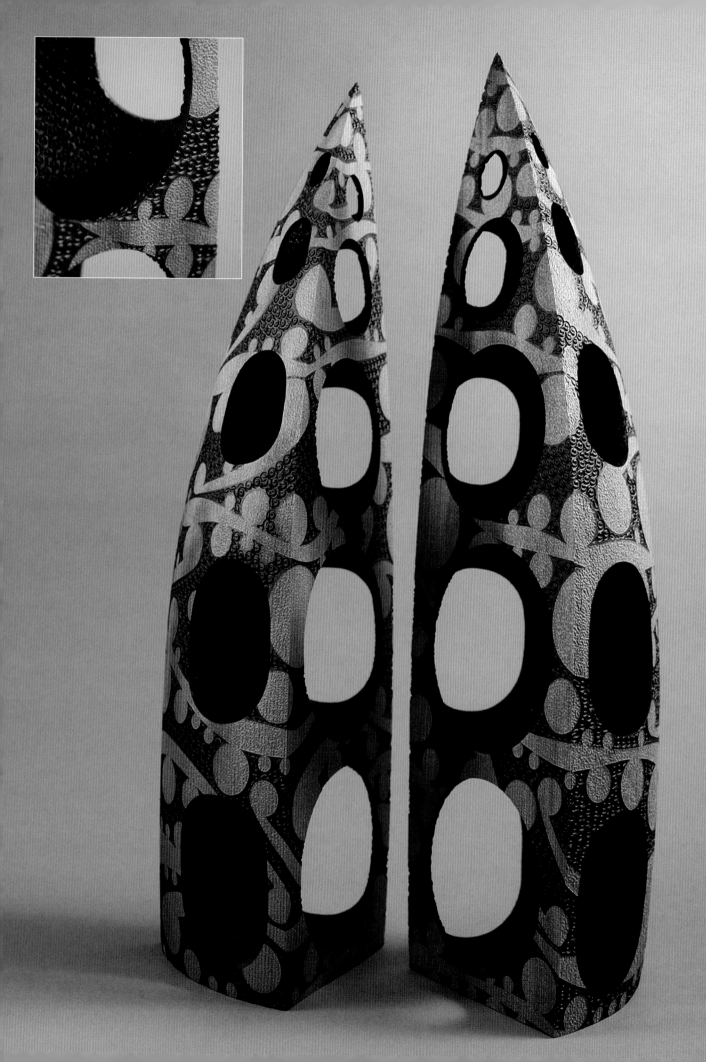

GRAEME PRIDDLE

Pacific Island Culture and the Ocean's Beauty

In 1989, New Zealander Graeme Priddle took voluntary retirement from work as a radio technician with the intention of starting a new lifestyle. In the early '90s, he bought a 100-acre property covered in native forest and with an abundance of deadfall logs from earlier logging operations. With a seemingly endless supply of wood, Priddle intended to make free-form furniture. As he

---

It is still a challenge to consistently come up with fresh ideas, so I tend to evolve an idea into a series of work.

---

explains, he never intended to be a wood turner. "A local furniture maker who was struggling to make a living in New Zealand's limited market introduced me to the Whangarei Studio Woodturners Guild. I attended one of their meetings, saw their work, and then watched a video of David Ellsworth in action. I was hooked."

For many turners around the world, Priddle's lifestyle would be a dream. Priddle resides in his quiet valley

in Hikurangi with his wife and three children. Priddle's workshop is surrounded by native forest and between trips abroad, he keeps in contact with the broader wood art community through the Internet.

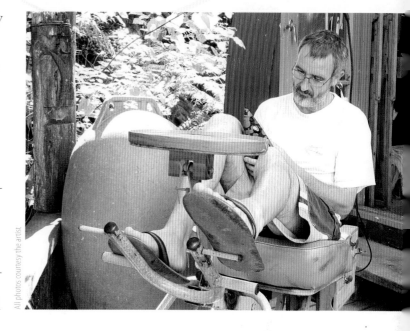

All photos, courtesy the artist

ABOVE

Priddle sits in a recycled and modified weight-training chair while he carves and textures his work.

OPPOSITE

Tahi Rua (One Two), 2007. Matai, acrylic paint; 15" high. Priddle developed the series, which suggests Polynesian canoes, when he was abroad on a residency and was suffering from homesickness. "I wanted to go home, but I didn't want to fly. I kept dreaming about sailing a boat home."

LEFT

The view through the end of *Tahi Rua* is astonishing because it so accurately reflects the end-on view through the diminishing compartments of a boat, even though it was all formed on the lathe. Priddle spent years racing centerboard yachts.

Priddle lives conveniently close to Ngahau Beach.

An Energetic Working Style

Priddle has mastered most of the techniques he needs, although he thinks it is important to keep up with creative and technological developments. He admits his working style is energetic. "The way I work tends to have two speeds—flat out and stop!" Nowadays he has found creative challenges are what keep him sharp. "It took many years of frustration producing bowls before I started to find my own voice. It is still a challenge to consistently come up with fresh ideas, so I tend to evolve an idea into a series of work."

Priddle has developed a signature style that has taken his pieces to collections around the world. When you look at a Priddle piece, there is no mistaking who the artist is. Part carved vessel, part patterned burning, part Maori, part environmental statement: the result is work that has a sense of place and pride that is unmatched.

Although he is mainly self-taught, along the way he has been inspired by many people, both within and outside the field he now has such a strong presence in. "Apart from my parents, who instilled in

The way I work has two speeds— flat out and stop!

me the belief I can do anything, my earliest influences were the Maori carvers whose work I saw in museums and wharenui (meeting houses). I am still strongly influenced by traditional carving and contemporary Maori art, as it is usually influenced by the environment, people and beliefs, which are the main things from which I draw inspiration."

Until he could support his family from his turning, he milled deadfall timber on his property. Now, he pays all of the bills through selling his art work. It should be ideal, but there are unanticipated problems, as Priddle explains: "During a working day, the main obstacles to getting in serious shop time are keeping up with the constantly changing needs of a family with three young adults and a grandson, looking after the property and house, and more and more e-mail. Also, the remoteness of our property means a trip to town for anything is a half-day affair. All of these things certainly influence each other and working from home means I am always on call. I started woodturning so I could spend more time at home with my young family. Little did I know a quiet life at home making wooden bowls would make me such a busy man."

Priddle resides what he calls a "spitting distance from the coast" and that is also a major source of inspiration for him. It is not hard to see these influences in his work. The bindings on his Starfish Vessels are reminiscent of the lashings the Polynesians used to build canoes that brought the Maori people to New Zealand. The swirling patterns carved into the wood and the incorporation of seashell into his work are further reflections of the marine influence. The Maori extensively use shell in their own work and the patterns Priddle burns into his pieces suggest traditional Maori work. The most distinctive pieces Priddle makes are his canoe-like forms. The compellingly evocative pieces are remarkable contributions to the turning world, while their decoration is as clear a statement of cultural esteem as can be found in any turned work anywhere.

Priddle has enjoyed the influence of other New Zealand turners. "During my early years as a wood turner I was drawn to the work of Rolly Munro (page 57), Alby Hall, and John Ecuyer, as they were all using turned forms as a starting point for sculptural objects and they also drew on our South Pacific environment and culture as sources of inspiration," he said. "I have always been drawn to the more sculptural and story-telling aspects of turning, and there are many, many other turners whose work has excited or inspired me for many different reasons."

ABOVE LEFT

Priddle marks a series of diminishing circles along a block of wood he plans to saw into a shape like a canoe prow, for the series of pieces he calls "waka." Each circle will become a turning center.

ABOVE RIGHT

Priddle turns a smaller waka off-center on his enormous lathe. He has already hollowed the piece on three centers and here cuts the fourth center. Once he has completed the turning, the piece will be ready for extensive carving.

LEFT

Priddle has developed a technique of tightly spaced branding using a coiled tip on a wood-burning tool. It burns and textures at the same time. He brushes the ash from the surface so he can see what is happening.

The Special Magic of Wood

Like many others, wood holds a special magic for Priddle. "The thing I like most about wood is it is a warm material to work with and it is not manufactured, so every piece is like a recorded slice of history. Also, the fact I have an endless supply on my property is a bonus, but I do purchase some timber for projects for which I don't have suitable wood."

In what has almost become a standard development for woodturners, Priddle started out emphasizing the natural beauty of timber. Now, although the lathe still defines the initial form, design is the dominant factor. After turning, he extensively carves most of his pieces. Priddle explains, "The lathe is definitely my most important tool, but these days probably about ten percent of the time on a piece is lathe work and the rest is carving, texturing and sanding with hand and power tools."

One of Priddle's most significant achievements has been the establishment of a charitable trust to promote and organize collaborative art and craft events in New Zealand. Inspired by the Emma Lake events in Saskatchewan, Canada, which he attended in 1996, CollaboratioNZ was held in Whangarei for the first time in 1998 and has been held every two years since then, with Priddle as the driving force behind the event. He also has been given the unique distinction of having one of his pieces featured on a New Zealand postage stamp. Certainly New Zealand culture and the world of wood art are much richer for his presence.

www.graemepriddle.co.nz

ABOVE

Point Break, 2006. Monterey cypress, mulga, copper, metallic thread; 8½" high x 6" wide x 3½" deep. Priddle first became known internationally for these carved vessels, which he says are inspired by his interest in the Pacific environment and people.

OPPOSITE

Starfish Vessel, 2006. Kauri, mulga, paua shell, copper; 22½" high x 5½" wide x 5½" deep. Priddle explains the series: "The carved and textural elements represent waves that wash the shore, rock textures, lichens, water patterns and the starfish, driftwood, and multitudes of shells left behind by receding tides. The apparent fragility of the vessels also conveys my concern our fragile marine environments are under constant threat."

BINH PHO

Stories Told with Color

Binh Pho tells stories with his work and he is one of the few woodturners today who focuses largely on autobiographical themes. The journey from his childhood in Vietnam to life as a woodturner in the United States is one of struggle and perseverance, yet he views it as a philosophical acceptance of destiny through the lens of

---

As an artist, my mission is to reveal the beauty and, in some way, exalt the life record of a once-living organic thing... to allow it to live again in a new way.

---

the happiness and success he found in the United States. In Pho's work, the difficulties he has faced in life are transformed through a unique aesthetic language. He sees how each of his experiences is connected, with the most difficult doors opening to future blessings. His work is his means of sharing this. A love of color, Eastern imagery and modern art are obvious in his pieces. While Asian iconography often appears,

All photos courtesy the artist

ABOVE

Pho handholds the piece while he creates its myriad tiny details.

LEFT

The sun sets over Pho's back porch railing in the midst of the Northern Illinois winter.

OPPOSITE

Rickshaw Park, 2007. Box elder, acrylic paint, dye, gold leaf; 13" high x 8" diameter. Pho's father told him stories of his childhood, when the rickshaw puller would take him to the park and then visit with the other pullers, with their rickshaws all lined up.

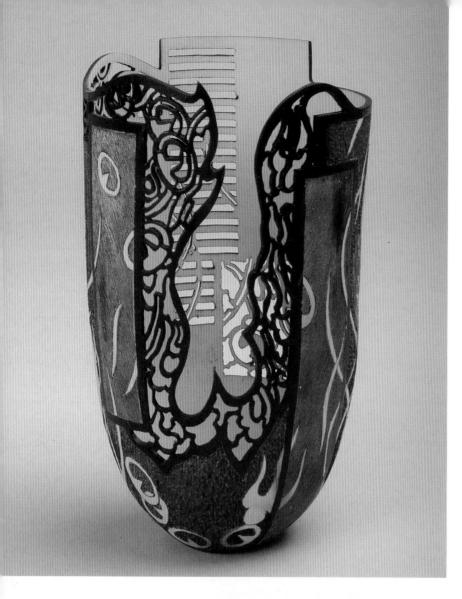

traditional Asian approaches to painting or working with wood are rare because Pho's work grew largely from the international field of artistic woodturning.

An early breakthrough in Pho's work was meeting the Canadian woodturner, Frank Sudol, at the Arrowmont School of Arts and Crafts. Sudol's piercing and airbrushing techniques opened a new world of self-expression for Pho. He combined the techniques with lessons learned from other woodturners: the use of color as employed by Giles Gilson and Michael Hosaluk (page 75), a sense of continuity learned from Michael Mode (page 81), and the use of metal leaf in the work of furniture maker David Marks. He's also influenced by the twentieth century Surrealist painters and sculptors, notably Salvador Dali and Mihail Chemiakin. Using the new approaches, and drawing upon his thoughts, memories and myths, Pho discovered his artistic potential.

ABOVE

Dream of Fire, 2007. Box elder, acrylic paint, gold leaf; 5" high x 2¾" diameter. Though *Dream of Fire* is small enough to cup in your hand, lush images cover it on all sides.

RIGHT

Dreamer, 2007. Bradford pear, acrylic paint, gold leaf; 4½" high x 3" diameter. Pho often creates small-scale works, despite the challenges involved. "Even in the small scale of work, all the details still need to be there," he explains. "It is more challenging to scale down the detail, working with a magnifying glass."

No Way Out, 2007. Citrus wood, acrylic paint and dye; 6" high x 3¾" diameter. *No Way Out* depicts a butterfly trapped in a dense bamboo forest near a stream, based on the story of Pho's capture by the Communists in Vietnam during an escape attempt.

How Pho Works: Start with a Turned Form

While Pho is known as a woodturner, he views turning as simply a means of creating forms to express three-dimensional imagery. Only 10 percent of Pho's time is spent working on the lathe, with the other 90 percent taken up by painting, piercing, and gilding the work. Turning the forms to a wall thickness of $\frac{1}{16}$" to $\frac{3}{32}$" enables him to pierce the design easily later. To gauge the wall

---

I use plain woods because I paint and pierce the surface, but when the wood has a lot of character I try to marry the natural figure and the design, but it is challenging. Wood is the tree's history.

---

thickness when he is turning, he shines a light on the far side of the translucent bowl body. When the light is uniform, so is the thickness. Because the walls are so thin, the turnings dry quickly—two to four weeks—depending on the humidity level. Once a bowl is dry, Pho can hand-sand it and move on to painting and detailing in his unique style.

For surface design, Binh Pho uses three main techniques: airbrushing, piercing/texturing, and gilding. Each technique produces a particular effect, and when he uses them in combination, the results can be stunningly beautiful. After he has turned the piece, Pho works directly on the surface with a pencil, marking out the areas he wishes to paint. After completing the sketch, he applies masking to cover some sections of the vessel while he lays down color or dye using a sophisticated airbrush

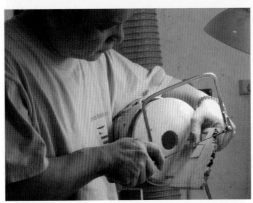

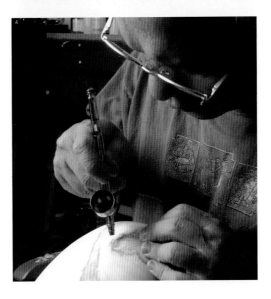

ABOVE

An adept woodturner, Pho typically reduces the walls of his forms to $\frac{3}{32}$" or thinner, but he says turning is only 10 percent of the work in a piece.

LEFT TOP

Pho uses the lathe as an armature to hold the work while he carefully saws the shapes he wants.

LEFT BOTTOM

Pho uses a tiny airbrush to apply color onto the wood.

that gives him control over line width, color intensity and gradation in a single stroke. He works mainly with acrylics, which are versatile, reliable, dry quickly, and can be transparent when properly thinned. The transparent color allows the grain of the wood to show through, a desirable effect

human life. "As a tree grows, the challenges it faces become part of its character," he says. "I usually use plain woods because I paint and pierce the surface, but when I get a piece of wood with a lot of character I try to marry the natural figure and the design, but it is challenging. Wood is the tree's history. When the whole tree dies, the form it made in life endures for a while, then decays, goes back to soil, and is forgotten. As an artist, my mission is to reveal the beauty and, in some way, exalt the life record of a once-living organic thing... to allow it to live again in a new way."

Pho's friendship with his fellow artists and the respect they have for his work often leads to collaborations. Sometimes the collaborations involve a process of planning, while at other times an artist will entrust him with a piece, counting on his unique vision and process to make it into something special.

Pho grew up in Saigon during the Vietnam War. His childhood memories are for the most part pleasant, though he remembers the horrors of the Tet Offensive and other fearful moments. During his college years, he witnessed the fall of Saigon, and then spent a year in a prison camp. Today, he is living his version of the American dream, enjoying a home and studio in the Illinois countryside with his wife and children. The long voyage that brought him to this place continues to be reflected in his works. He has earned a reputation as a good friend and talented artist among collectors, gallery owners, and his peers. Those who have come to know his family consider him a fortunate man as well.

www.wondersofwood.net

since the character of the wood remains an important aspect of Pho's work. Once all of the artwork has been colored, Pho removes the masking and begins to pierce the walls. Occasionally he gilds the surface with metal leaf in combination with piercing, to create a wonderfully rich effect.

From his first explorations in wood, Pho was driven by a philosophical bent and by his desire to share his deep respect for nature. He selected wood as his principal medium because he believes it mirrors

Occasionally, Pho uses his talents to tell the experiences of others. A wonderful example is *Tears of the Phoenix*, which he began two years ago. He bumped his tool against the rim of the vessel as the lathe was winding down. The result was devastating—the vessel broke in two. He set it aside for two years, until a studio visitor asked if he ever broke any pieces. "Yes, of course," Pho replied. "But normally I cut them up and do something with them—except this one." The visitor asked him to complete the piece, but Pho explained the repaired piece would not be good enough. The man persisted, and told Binh a story:

The man's daughter, Kari, had been in a terrible accident and had spent a long time in a coma. It seemed there was no hope for her recovery but she eventually did wake up and recovered. Pho was being asked to create a piece from his broken vessel to celebrate her new life.

"Instead of joining the pieces together where it was broken, I shifted the bottom 90 degrees to show the defective part on the front as the main feature," Pho says. "I used three main braces to join the broken vessel at the bottom to the perfect top."

The number three represents healing as well as heaven, earth, and man. Because Kari was born in the year of the Wood Hare, Pho airbrushed the blurred shadow of the hare by the defective part of the vessel. On the back, he placed a negative image of the Phoenix, representing rebirth. The year of the accident and Kari's rebirth was the year of the Water Rooster, so the image on top of the vessel is a water rooster raised above everything else. He also added teardrop imagery to the three braces, as the parent had written a book about the experience titled *Laughing Through the Tears*.

For the lid, Pho carved a piece of wood in the shape of a healing rock that fits in the palm, using Kari's favorite colors. Her name was etched in the top and base of the piece, along with the Chinese character for 'tear.' He also expanded the vessel opening a little more, shaped it like an eye, and added one more teardrop there. After much consideration, the title came to him: *Tears of the Phoenix*.

Pho uses a powered carving tool to pierce the walls of *Tears of the Phoenix*.

To create a lid, Pho carved and painted a healing rock that fits into the palm of the hand.

Tears of the Phoenix, 2006. Box elder burl, acrylic paint and dye; 14" high x 7" diameter. The image of the hare appears in the airbrushed color on the right front of the vase form.

On the back of the piece, Pho has pierced the image of the phoenix rising from the flames.

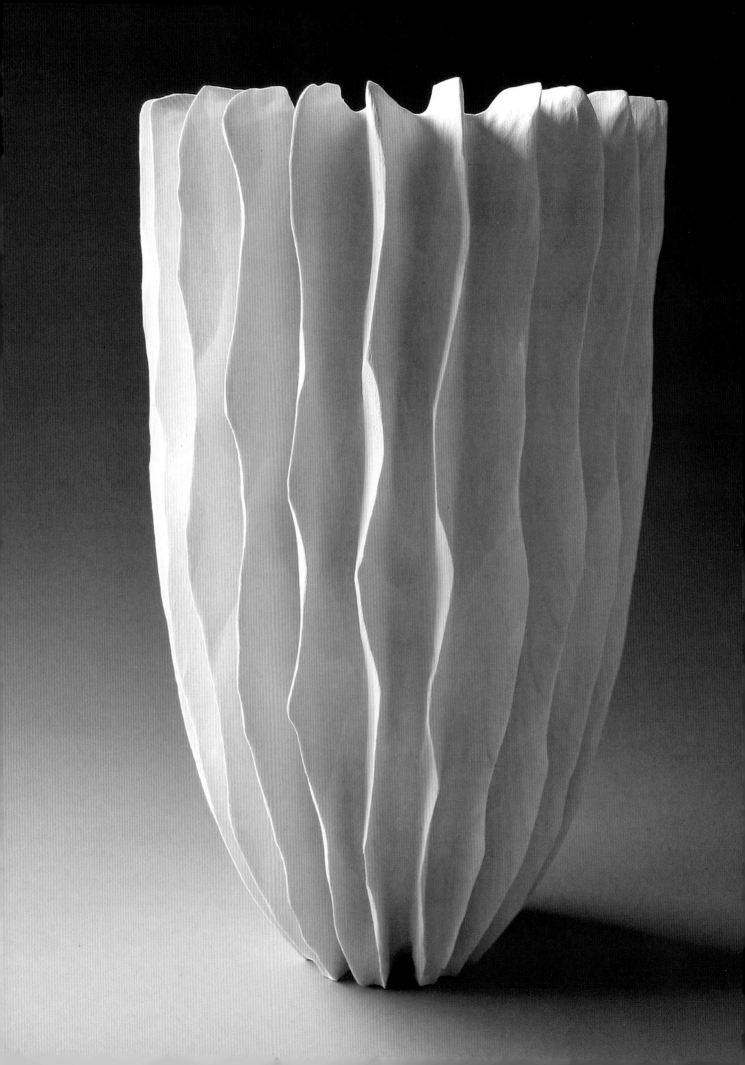

MARC RICOURT

The Vessel Was Mankind's First Tool

Like many other contemporary turners, the career path of the French artist Marc Ricourt was indirect. His interest in wood began when he decided he wanted to be a cabinet maker, but once he achieved that goal his creative urge led him to the Beaux-Arts school in Dijon to learn to draw. Ricourt spent much of his time there

---

The vessel is a wonderful concept—useful, yet mysterious. I try to find harmony between the wood, the shape, texture, and color.

---

developing new techniques, such as applying plaster to canvas to achieve a textured effect. What he did not realize was the search for three-dimensional effects would lead to woodturning.

"One day, I saw a used lathe in a store and thought it might be a way to combine working in wood with my love of texture," he says. "With a little help from a friend and some books I started to play with it. I was happy I had found a way to work in three dimensions, but I didn't know what it would lead to."

A kind of harmony developed between Ricourt's lifestyle and his new-found passion for turning. He bought a 200-year-old stone house which suited his needs perfectly, as he describes: "My house is in a little village with only forty inhabitants. It is in the Burgundy region near Dijon where the landscape is beautiful and there are lots of forests. In fact, 95 percent of my wood comes from the area. My house used to belong a clog

All photos courtesy the artist

ABOVE

Ricourt deeply carves a piece with a die grinder while it is still on the lathe.

OPPOSITE

Vessel, 2007. Bleached ash; 17½" high x 10" diameter. The fins on the deeply carved piece approach translucence at the edges, shading the light and softening the whole impression.

maker, so it is nice that it is being used for woodwork again."

Ricourt continued to develop his ideas in isolation, although he was influenced by others' work. "The English turner Mike Scott was the first, then David Ellsworth (page xi). I also like the sculpture of David Nash and Constantin Brancusi." Eventually,

---

My house used to belong a clog maker, so it is nice that it is being used for woodwork again.

---

he found the wider world of turning. In 2000, he attended the World Turning Conference in Puy-St-Martin in the south of France and met many established turners, some of whom suggested he should try his luck in the United States, so in 2001, he traveled there. "I visited many major collectors and saw hundreds of pieces of wood art. In France, a woodturner is considered an artisan, but over there a woodturner is an artist. It was just what I needed to change my life."

RIGHT

Ricourt uses a gouge to carve deep texture in the surface of a sawn turning to create a paired sculpture.

BELOW TOP

Vessel, 2006. Ash; 18" high x 7½" diameter. In his endless exploration of the textured surface, Ricourt contrasts regularity with roughness, sharpness and softness. His pieces trap the light, creating intriguing shadows.

Exploring the Vessel

In recent years, Ricourt has concentrated on exploring the vessel. "I think the vessel was the first tool created and used by mankind. I find it a wonderful concept— useful, yet mysterious. I try to find harmony between the wood, the shape, texture, and color. In my mind, there is a symbolic feeling to the work." His pieces often give the impression of remote cultures or lost civilizations and he admits to a fascination with many traditional art forms, from Oceania to Africa, and from the Bronze Age to the present.

Just watching Ricourt work is exhausting. Like many other creative turners today, turning accounts for only a part of the work. After hollowing and shaping the outside of a vessel on the lathe, he then energetically attacks it with a variety of power carving tools. "I use the lathe for all my pieces," he says, "but the shaping and hollowing only account for about thirty per cent. Seventy percent of the work is carving the outside."

Ricourt enhances his work with such robust texturing that it is sometimes hard to recognize it was ever turned or even that it is wood. Many woodturners hold the vessel they have turned in such reverence that they only tentatively rework it, unwilling to destroy the purity of line or the beautiful wood figure. Not Ricourt. He deeply carves, sometimes incising grooves so far that they break through the walls of the vessel, allowing peep-views of the interior. In other works, he carves spiraling grooves that swirl around the vessel, lifting and energizing the piece. He makes no attempt to hide the tool marks, but the roughness belies the control required to make such consistent cuts. When the carving is done, he bleaches, sandblasts, dyes, stains, sands, and further roughens the work until the original vessel is barely recognizable. Often his pieces look wholly organic, with a softness to the finish

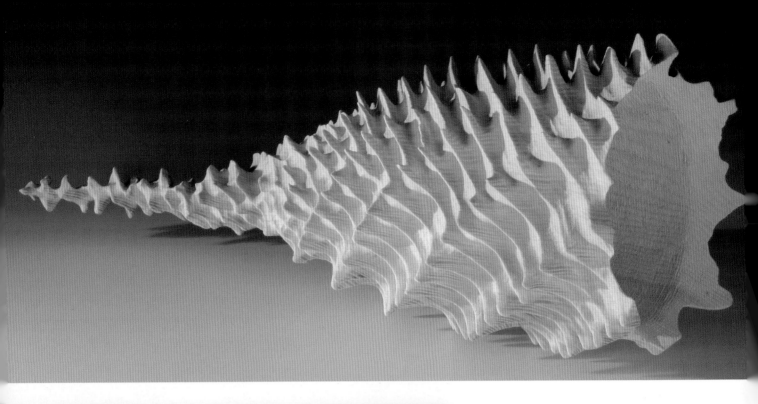

that makes them appear to be the work of nature. Whatever is in his mind, Ricourt does not name his pieces, leaving viewers free to create their own fantastic stories.

Ricourt gives the impression he has unlimited ideas to translate into solid works. Certainly he puts in a lot of time

---

I saw a used lathe and thought it might be a way to combine working in wood with my love of texture. I didn't know what it would lead to.

---

to realize these ideas, up to ten hours per day in the well-equipped workshop. His enormous lathe enables him to turn large, thick-walled pieces. He can then rotate the work while it is still on the lathe, carving his trademark deep textures. Afterwards he refines the carving on his work bench beside a high window which floods the work with natural light. His lifestyle in his beautiful home reflect his passion for art, wood, and traditional values.

www.marcricourt.errance.net

ABOVE TOP

Vessel, 2007. Bleached ash; 25" long x 10" diameter. In a rare departure from Ricourt's upright vases, this reclining piece resembles the carapace of a beached sea creature.

ABOVE BOTTOM

Vessel, 2006. Pear; 9" high x 11" diameter.

OPPOSITE

Vessel, 2006. Walnut and ferrous oxide; 18" high x 6" diameter. *Vessel* reveals the carving-away process whereby Ricourt reduces the diameter of the turned piece with deep texturing. The cascading grooves create a sense of movement.

MIKE LEE

Wood Is a Joy To Work or My Worst Nightmare

The works of Michael Lee harmonize form, gesture, and texture with abstract forms inspired by his experience of nature. He begins working on a new piece with a sense of the shape, but relies largely upon intuition as the work develops. The sculptural forms that result from the process make it clear how much his natural environment affects his work.

Lee was born and raised on the Hawaiian island of Oahu. "It's a great place to live and raise a family," he says. "For an artist, it offers a laid-back lifestyle, as well as a very stimulating place to work, with beautiful green mountains and the warm blue waters of the Pacific Ocean. My favorite surf spot is just ten minutes away so it's easy for me to grab a quick session, as well as gather information for my next piece."

While surfing as a means of doing research for his work might seem a stretch, the influence of the sea and the coast is obvious in Lee's work. If his pieces seem surreal or haunting, there is a reason for that as well. Lee is perhaps the only woodturning artist who points to the writer Stephen King as an influence. "His books

Photo courtesy the artist. Other photos by Hugo de Vries unless otherwise indicated.

ABOVE

Lee lives on the Hawaiian island of Oahu, where he surfs daily as preparation for his work in wood. He enjoys spending time in the ocean with his children, Kassidy and Kaiana.

LEFT

Koolina lagoon is the beach where I often spend time with my family, swimming, diving or just hanging out to watch the sunset," Lee says.

OPPOSITE

Object Of Our Affection, 2006. Gabon ebony, fine silver, 3" high x 5" wide x 11" deep. "Our son turned 13 last year and as I reflected on this milestone, I had a desire to capture the moment he was born," Lee says. "*Object Of Our Affection* represents a family portrait of my wife and I, as starfish vessels, cradling our first-born."

Photo courtesy the artist

RIGHT

Our House, 2005. Kamani, kingwood, yellowheart, padauk, Gabon ebony, lignum vitae; 6½" long x 11" wide x 10½" deep. "*Our House* is a family portrait in which our *ohana* is nestled in their humble abode," Lee says. "Our house always has been a place of refuge and comfort for me and my family."

BELOW

Celestial Seasons, 2005. Koa, gabon ebony, padauk, yellowheart, lignum vitae, various gold leaf, 4½" high x 10" wide x 11" deep. "I wanted to convey the changing of the seasons by using the different colors of wood for the pods and further enhancing them with various shades of gold leaf," Lee says. "The brown tones of the bowl laced with the sapwood clouds represent mother earth cradling her celestial seasons."

have allowed my imagination to expand and explore options in my work in a surreal manner," Lee explains. Lee's unique aesthetic also is due to the early impact of jade and ivory carvings his mother brought with her from China. "These pieces were my first introduction to the world of carving."

Lee originally became involved with woodturning because he was dissatisfied with his career in the computer field. "To prevent myself from being bored silly, I decided to buy a lathe, a book, and a set of turning tools. I proceeded to teach myself

---

I design my carved pieces around the fact they will be turned in some way or another first, and the turning remains an important aspect and serves as the focal point for the rest of the piece.

---

the fine art of bludgeoning wood." With time, Lee became "addicted to turning" and was skilled enough to sell his work part-time at local craft fairs. Working as a studio assistant at Arrowmont School of Arts and Crafts gave him a close look at many well-known woodturners, making it clear to him that the craft had potential as an art form.

In contrast with the formal education at Arrowmont and immersion in woodturning, which was exciting, Lee was increasingly unhappy with his day job. He decided to attempt making a living as a full-time woodturner and found a way to make it work, balancing the creation of Hawaiian calabash bowls and small vessels for the tourist market with one-of-a-kind sculptural works exhibited by leading galleries. "I love being my own boss and making things with my hands. When I was in the computer field, I was just a little cog in a wheel. As a woodturner, I can go into my studio, turn something, and have that tangible object to admire and hold in my hands at the end of the day. There is a real sense of satisfaction and contentment to being a woodturner."

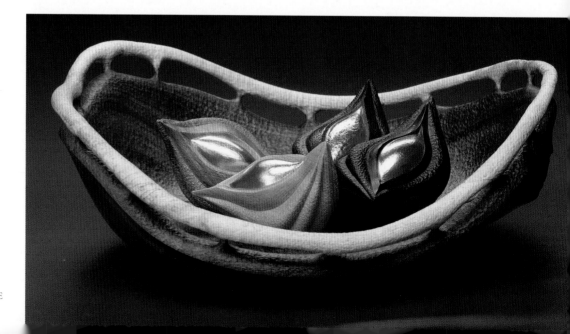

Start the Day Surfing

Lee employs the lathe early in the process of creating his sculptural pieces but there is often little evidence of woodturning in the final product. "For straight production bowls and vessels, pretty much all of the work is defined by the lathe, with the exception of some light texturing. The carved pieces require much more extensive work off the lathe, although the portion done by the lathe is crucial to the overall effect of the finished piece. I design my carved pieces around the fact they will be turned in some way or another first, and the turning remains an important aspect and serves as the focal point for the rest of the piece."

Lee fully embraces the quality of life for which Hawaii is known. He believes going surfing in the morning is the best way to start his working day and listening to music is important to the carving process. "I'll put my headphones on with some good music and just start carving," he says. "After that, a lot of it is intuitive. Often a couple of hours will fly by and I'll look down at the piece and not even know how I got there. I usually don't have a right or wrong answer to the direction of a piece I'm working on. During the course of a day, I will have several different design detours tugging at me. Sometimes, the decisions are directly related to the limitations of my tools, so a curve or line may take a different turn than first intended."

While working on a piece, Lee usually cradles it his hands, turning it over and examining it as it evolves. Lee tends to work on a scale conducive to the process, which provides a sense of intimacy and results in tactile and visually seductive

www.leewoodart.com

works. "I always have enjoyed the warmth of wood," Lee says of his chosen medium. "The different smells, densities and colors of wood all contribute to my love of it. Wood can be either a joy to work or my worst nightmare, but in the end it's the unpredictability that makes it such an exciting material with which to work."

Ohana, 2004. Lignum vitae, milo, Gabon ebony, koa, yellowheart; 4" long x 4" wide x 3½" deep, to 2" long x 2" wide x 1¾" deep. "*Ohana* means family in Hawaiian," Lee says. "The piece is a family portrait representing me, my wife, Debbie, son, Zachary, and daughters, Kassidy and Kaiana."

Brood, 2005. Cocobolo rosewood, Gabon ebony, tagua nuts, 3½" high x 6" wide x 8" deep. Says Lee, "*Brood* represents my ongoing fascination with family, fossils, and fantasy. A mother crab dutifully guards her nest of eggs."

ALAIN MAILLAND

There Is No Limit to the Forms I Can Make

In a field where work is prized for its originality, most contemporary woodturners would agree the most difficult thing is to come up with new ideas about how to bend the limits of the lathe and create unique work. Of the artists who have developed new ways to use the lathe, no one is more creative than the French artist

When I need a new tool, I fire up my forge and make the tool.

Alain Mailland. He manages to generate ideas faster than anyone else does and the only limits seem to be the time it takes to make them and the stress on his body that comes from long hours of intensive work. With a worldwide reputation as a creative wood artist, Mailland is not only a turning genius, but also a sculptor of rare talent. His works defy the imagination, because the forms he produces are largely created on the lathe using mounting and turning techniques unmatched anywhere in the world.

Mailland was born in Paris, but it was too grey for him, so now he lives near Uzes in the sunny south of France on two acres covered in natural bush. With the skills learned in an earlier life as a carpenter, mason, and roofer, he built his own house out of local stone. "I bought a ruin and built a home," he proudly states. Next, he dug his workshop into the rocky side of the hill, which keeps the partly underground space warmer in winter and cooler in the fierce summers. Light

All photos courtesy the artist unless otherwise indicated

ABOVE

Mailland enjoys a close look at one of his complex turnings.

OPPOSITE

Eureka, 2003. Hackberry, 21" high x 19½" diameter. It is easy to imagine Mailland struggling to solve the problem of how to make this piece. Its core explodes into flaring petal forms, just like the idea: "Eureka! I have it!"

RIGHT

Mailland dug his
workshop into the
side of a hill, so it's
cool in summer
and warm in winter.

BELOW

Mailland had this
enormous lathe made
to his specifications.
It has an 8 hp motor
and with four gears
can run at between
150 and 1,306
rpm. Including the
fabricated bed, the
lathe weighs 1,320
pounds, which helps
damp vibrations
when he turns
off-center pieces.

streams in through wide windows on one side and a skylight in the roof. Recently Mailland purchased a 10-acre property in the mountains with an old farmhouse, a spring, two rivers, chestnut trees, and wild boars, and he plans to move there in the near future.

From an early age Mailland liked to paint and was influenced by the work of the Impressionist masters. For someone who appears to see the world differently than most of us, this was an important influence. Mailland explains: "They gave me the idea that your world is only as it is because of the way you look at it." He also was very influenced by the world of plants from an early age. "I used to study plants with my mother. We collected them and made a herbarium. I now see that this period of observation was really important for what I do, because I looked closely at the natural forms and their structures. Now I make these forms, so I can say nature is also my teacher."

A Wide Range of Skills

Mailland works intuitively from his observations of nature and through his own explorations as he draws. It is not always an easy path, as he explains: "I started to make my flower shapes in 1996. It was a real technical challenge. I had to learn blacksmithing, and I spent two weeks designing and making the tools I needed. Then I had to find the right wood. When all of that was done, I was able to make the flower shapes I produce now for my sculptures. These days, there is no limit to the forms I can make. When I need a new tool, I fire up my forge and make the tool."

Not satisfied with the complexity of the forms, Mailland has also developed a range of skills in carving, steam-bending, texturing, and other techniques. Perhaps his most spectacular innovations have been the remarkable chucking systems he has developed to create eccentric turnings. "I started to explore it in 1998 and have never stopped. With different technical challenges each time, I use different systems for holding the piece on the lathe—wooden chucks, wedges, screws, chains, straps—sometimes I've turned sixty centers on one piece."

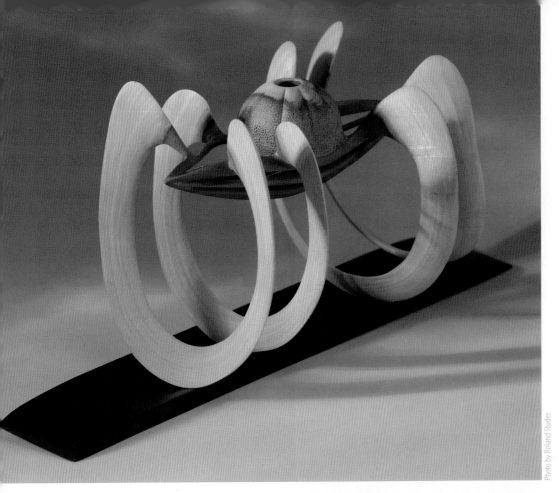

Photo by Roland Studer

Solar Ship, 2007.
Lignum vitae; 6" long
x 5" diameter. The
circular rims of *Solar Ship*
supporting the central
vessel were turned on
the long axis and their
centers were carved away.
The piece was rotated 90
degrees and rechucked
to turn the central vessel.
The boat form under the
vessel was wholly carved.

Trio, 2004. Pistachio;
11" high x 7¾" diameter.
Inverting what we might
expect, Mailland makes
the bird-mouthed vessels
into the base of *Trio*.
Are they wings or tails
at the top? They can be
anything you like. It's hard
to believe such a complex
form can be turned and
carved from a single
piece of wood.

Usually Mailland does the preliminary work on a piece, and then leaves it to dry for some time. "First I do the woodturning and the carving, mostly in green wood. Then I let the piece dry. I have to keep an eye on it and control the distortions by slowing down

Sometimes I get a great piece of wood from my friend the forester and I immediately see what I can do with it, so I start straight away.

the drying process if necessary. When the piece is dry, I do the final carving, sanding, texturing, sandblasting, bending, and so on. Sometimes a piece can wait several years before I finish it, although I occasionally get a great piece of wood from my friend the forester and I immediately see what I can do with it, so I start straight away."

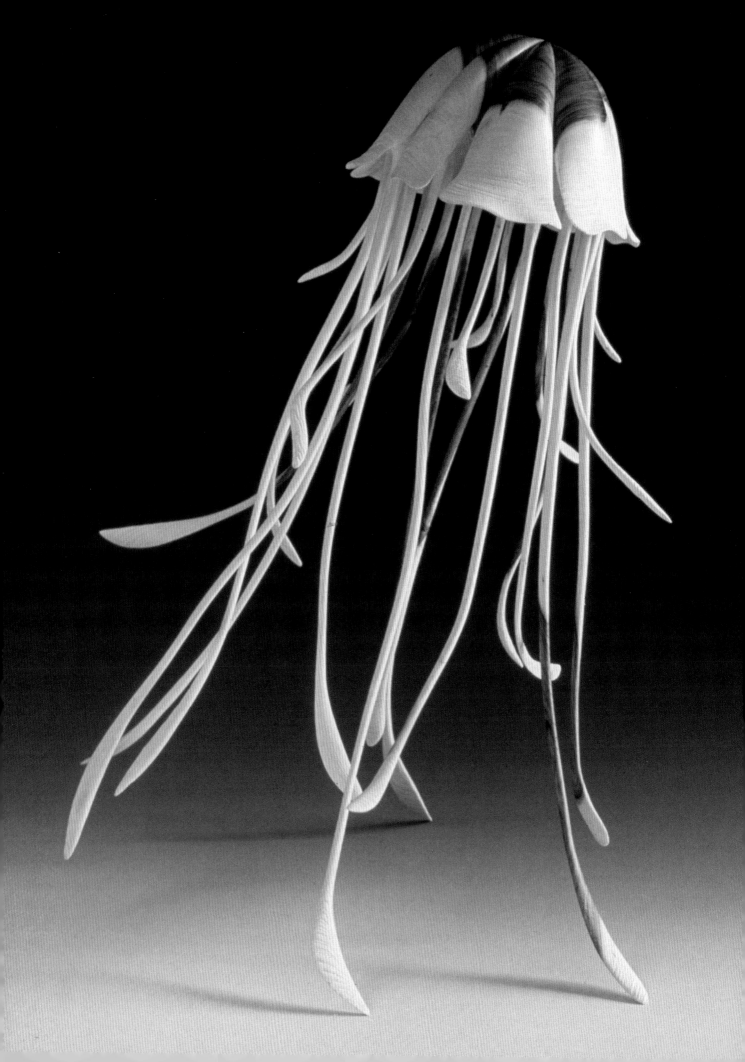

The Universe Is Made of Circles

The actual turning accounts for only about 10 to 20 percent of the work Mailland does on a piece, while the carving is about 20 to 40 percent. The rest of the time is spent sanding, texturing, sandblasting, or finishing. However, Mailland is in no doubt about the importance of the lathe in his work. "Even if I spend so much more time carving and sanding, the lathe is the most important tool in my work, because, except for a few pieces, they all start with the turning. It is a magical process that gives a center to the piece and allows you to make hollow forms. Everything in the universe is made with circular elements, from cells and atoms to galaxies, so I keep close to nature by using the lathe."

Mailland's respect for nature extends to the wood itself and his respect for the material is intense. "It can take hundreds of years

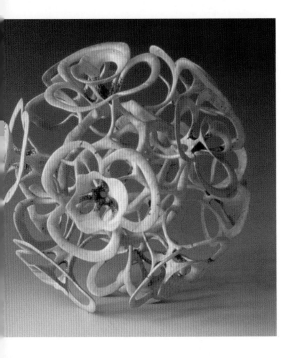

I Had a Dream, 2006. Arbutus (madrone) root; 5½" diameter. Though it is difficult to determine which parts of the complex piece were turned and which were carved, Mailland maintains the lathe remains the essential center of his work.

to make a piece of wood. When you hold it in your hand, it is like you have received the past as a gift. What a gift! Sometimes it takes two hundred years of patience from the tree, waiting for the rain, growing in the sun, sleeping in the cold of winter, making fruit…. I love the woods from my countryside, because they suffer from the droughts and the heat in summer. They are real treasures and feel I have to succeed with them as a sign of respect for their beauty."

It is impossible not to be moved by Mailland's sincerity. Everything he does is a heartfelt expression of his beliefs and he has little patience with those who do not respect the world as he does. Certainly he deserves our full respect and gratitude for his extraordinary contribution.

www.mailland.fr

ABOVE

Blob, 2001. Juniper burl; 10¾" high x 13½" diameter. It's difficult to imagine each one of these tiny vessels is hollowed on a different axis. The imagination required, first to conceive such a piece, then to make it possible, is extraordinary.

OPPOSITE

The Elegance of Pelagie. 2005. Pistachio; 11" high x 8" diameter. The extraordinary fluidity of Mailland's shapes seem particularly well suited to representing sea creatures.

Back to the Sea, 2006. Arbutus (madrone) root, 19¾" high x
9" diameter. To make *Back to the Sea*, Mailland had to remount
the burl root on the lathe to turn each of the small vase shapes.
Each one requires changing the orientation of the wood
in relation to the axis of rotation and to its position on the
chucking system.

Mailland uses an ingenious system of wedges and straps
to mount the irregular burl that will become *Back to the Sea*
on the lathe.

The lathe helps Mailland complete
the mouth and the hollow inside of
each vase form. At this point, he has
completed the turning of *Back to the Sea*
but there is a lot of carving to come.

Using a variety of hand and power tools, Mailland extensively carves *Back to the Sea*, to
separate and refine the vase forms.

Rainbowls, 2005. Hackberry, 36" x 4" x 9". To make *Rainbowls*, Mailland had to combine multicenter turning, carving, and wood bending.

Starting with a long and thick chunk of wood, Mailland band saws a blank and mounts it outboard to turn five chucking spigots and vase bases; three of them have been completed.

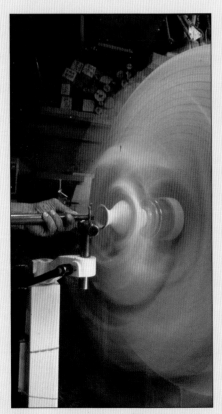

Mailland reverses the blank so he can mount each of the five spigots in the lathe chuck. Now he can hollow the insides of the five vessels, and turn the exterior of their mouths.

With the carving mostly completed, Mailland steams the wood and bends it over a curved form. After bending, he will carve the surface textures that enliven the completed piece.

DAVID SENGEL

Much Yet to Do with the Lathe

David Sengel keeps busy in many ways because he and his wife are small-scale organic farmers. One of Sengel's greatest pleasures is to walk though the garden each day, checking progress and relaxing with his plants. He explains: "I find it to be good therapy in its own right, not to mention a needed break from working in the

The variables in wood often affect the direction a form will take, and dealing with these challenges is most enjoyable.

studio. The good community of growers reminds me of the best aspects of the turning world. My involvement with farming may grow to include some agritourism, and I am hoping that may finally give me the impetus to make some larger outdoor pieces. I still can't believe I've never used the nine-and-a-half-foot length capacity of my old Oliver lathe."

Sengel's home is a calm haven and he takes pride in describing it. "I live and work on about twenty acres in the rural mountains of North Carolina, three hundred yards from the eastern continental divide. Where I live is an important part of who I am. We have a nineteenth century house that has been a woodworking project for twenty-five years, a workshop I built and have added on to numerous times, and various other outbuildings, ponds, and gardens. It is a comfortable environment, despite the high-upkeep. The workshop tends to be a bit cluttered because I have been frequenting metal scrap

All photos by Chuck Hearon

ABOVE

Sengel says, "We have a nineteenth century house that has been a woodworking project for 25 years, and a workshop that I built and have added on to numerous times."

OPPOSITE

Chamber of Woo, 2007. Black walnut, locust thorns; 13" high x 10" wide. The handle is adorned with threatening thorns and serves as a kind of anti-functional statement that fits in well with Sengel's sense of irony.

Lidded Vessel, 1996.
Dyed maple, locust, and
rose thorns; 12" high.
Another of Sengel's
thorn series. How would
you open a vessel so
dangerously barbed?

Recognized for Thorns

Sengel explains he "turned untutored for three years and made anything from simple bowls to clocks, but my technique couldn't take me where my imagination wanted to go." Classes with established wood artists took care of that, along with the unqualified sharing of ideas and techniques that characterizes the field. "Michael Peterson remains one of my favorite artists working in wood and I must admit my current heroes are sculptors who do not use a lathe. Some of them use few tools more technical than their hands and their imagination. These include Andy Goldsworthy and David Nash."

Beginning in 1991, Sengel became well known for his pieces incorporating thorns, an idea that came when another wood artist sent him some locust thorns from Arkansas. He produced many of the pieces throughout the '90s, exploring their potential in remarkable ways and firmly establishing himself as an artist. During this same period, he experimented with multi-axis turning. "The early bird forms were done this way just to see if I could make it work, though now they are mostly carved."

By 1998, Sengel believed his work was becoming predictable and found gluing thorns onto wood to be tedious. "I really hate to think how many thorns have passed through my hands," he says, "but it made my work identifiable I suppose." Around that time, he took stock of his life and started changing his priorities. "It is much easier these days to see what is important. Now I take more time to get out, be in, and observe the real world, the natural world."

yards for twenty-five years or more. Until recently, we averaged at least fifty inches of snow a year, but this wonderfully sculptural material has been all too scarce the past few winters."

As a child, Sengel was influenced by his father, who had a small woodworking shop in the basement. He remembers playing in the woodworking shop, something he still enjoys. Sengel studied piano repair in New York and for more than ten years had a business tuning and rebuilding pianos, developing many skills that have served him well in his later work. In the 1980s, when he was feeling the need to be more creative, he read some articles on the early resurgence of woodturning and decided to try his hand.

Fascination with Nature

Sengel's personal recentering gave him space to think about his work, and he grew determined to make pieces that meant more to him personally, which often means they reflect his fascination with nature. "One of the strongest influences on my work through the years has been the natural destructive forces in nature. Weathering, bleaching, rusting, the sculpting by insects, are all effects I admire and sometimes try to emulate."

These days Sengel tends to work on one piece at a time rather than in a related series, a process he admits slows the development of ideas. "More often than not, I begin work with an idea in mind, but then come up with a turned form that is essentially a blank canvas to be altered in some way. The variables in wood often affect the direction

Sweet Perch, 2007. Spalted maple, various thorns, glass insert; 20" high x 8" wide (excluding the flowers). Sengel combines his love of sculptural turning with his other love, horticulture. The flowers are real, the bird is not, but the bird is no less fascinated by the flowers. The bird's body is mostly turned.

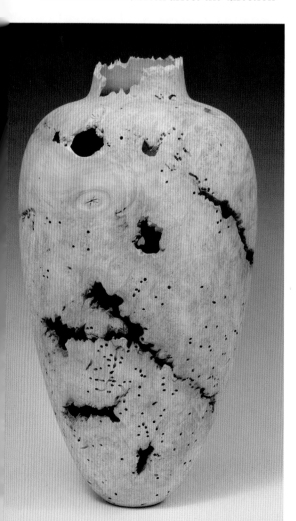

Vessel from the Ocean Floor, 2004. Maple burl; 18" high x 9" diameter. *Vessel from the Ocean Floor* is a nostalgic return to the kind of work Sengel made when he started turning.

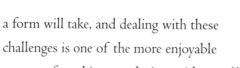

a form will take, and dealing with these
challenges is one of the more enjoyable
aspects of working, or playing, with wood."

As has been the case for many years,
Sengel continues to produce what he likes,
ignoring the pressures of commercial hype.
His work often reflects his pensive nature
and his love of the simple life. If he is
thinking of flowers, then why not put some
real flowers in his work? Sengel's work has
always challenged not only the individual
viewer, but also the field of turning and
wood art itself. His thorned work has
almost been a challenge to the whole idea
of collecting wood art: "Can you pick
me up? Let me see you try!" Never afraid
to make a political statement through
his work, Sengel continues to challenge

preconceived notions of what is both
possible and acceptable.

Sengel says, "Were it not a part of how
I make a living, I believe the extent of my
artistic pursuits would probably come
down to working with whatever materials
are here on this land, stacking rocks, tying
trees together, planting, ice and snow, etc.
However... I still love the turning process
and am secure in the knowledge there is
still much that has not been done with the
lathe." In 2000, Sengel said, "I have longed
for the freedom to make work without
having to care where it ends up, and the
process of giving myself that permission
continues." He seems to have found that
peaceful life, a balance between growing
plants and growing art.

GLOSSARY

Axis of Rotation
The line between the centers of the lathe's headstock and tailstock is its axis of rotation. Forms turned on a single axis of rotation are symmetrical about that axis.

Bleaching
Treating wood with a bleaching agent to remove the wood color. When oak is bleached it turns a chalky white color.

Burl
A round woody growth on the trunk of a tree, usually the result of entwined growth of numerous small buds, in which the grain is likely to run every which way. Wood artists prize burls because of the intricate color and figure they contain.

Chuck
A mechanical device for holding and mounting work on the driving end (headstock) of a lathe. Much of the innovation in contemporary woodturning has been greatly aided by recent developments in lathe chucks.

Ebonizing
Treating wood with a blackening agent to produce a deep and lustrous black color, or rather, absence of color.

Faceplate, Faceplate Turning
The faceplate is a heavy metal disk that threads onto the lathe headstock, permitting the secure attachment of a block of wood with or without additional support from the tailstock.

Gouge
A fluted chisel attached to a long handle, used to remove wood from the workpiece that is spinning on the lathe. Gouges are manufactured in a wide range of widths, from ¼" to 2", and with various amounts of curvature in the flute. The cutting tip of most gouges is formed by a single bevel ground on the outside (convex) of the flute.

Headstock
The powered end of the lathe, animated by an electric motor, to which the workpiece may be attached and by which the workpiece rotates.

Lathe
A machine for working a piece of wood, metal, or plastic by rotating it against a steel tool that shapes it by peeling away material. The lathe is singular among woodworking machines because it moves the wood against a hand-guided tool; most machinery uses a rotating cutter to remove material from a hand-guided piece of wood.

Multi-Axis Turning
By removing and remounting the workpiece, the turner may shape it on more than one axis of rotation. This can result in vessels with more than one opening, and turned objects that are non-symmetrical about a single axis.

Ornamental Turning
Ornamental turning refers to a nineteenth century set of tools and techniques that produces surfaces and forms featuring intricate decoration and engraving. The ornamental lathe uses an indexing headstock in combination with powered cutters guided by a mechanical tool armature. Contemporary wood artists recently have revived and expanded these techniques.

Skew, Skew Chisel
A turning chisel with a long handle and blade, the blade being flat in cross section with a sharp cutting end ground at an angle to the length of the tool. The cutting edge is formed by the intersection of two ground bevels.

Spalt, Spalted Wood, Spalting
When fungal decay both softens the wood and laces it with intricately shaped networks of dark lines, the wood is said to be spalt (spoilt). Spalted wood, typically maple or birch, is difficult to turn, but many wood artists value it for the patterns it reveals.

Tailstock
The passive end of a lathe, used to support a workpiece being driven by the powered headstock. Typically the tailstock can be moved along the lathe bed to accommodate work of different sizes.

ORGANIZATIONS

American Association of Woodturners
Larry Sommer, Executive Director
222 Landmark Center
75 W. Fifth St.
St Paul, MN 55102-1431
Phone: 651-484-9094
Fax: 651-484-1724
www.woodturner.org
The AAW is an international, non-profit organization dedicated to
the advancement of woodturning. Its mission is to provide education,
information, and organization to those interested in turning wood.

Woodturning Center
Albert LeCoff, Executive Director
501 Vine Street, Philadelphia, PA 19106 USA
Phone: 215-923-8000
Fax: 215-923-4403
www.woodturningcenter.org
The Wood Turning Center, a Philadelphia-based not-for-profit international
arts institution, gallery and resource center, supports and develops the field
of lathe-turned art.

Dutch Woodturners Association
www.houtdraaien.com

French Association for Artistic Woodturning
www.aftab-asso.com

Irish Woodturners Guild
www.irishwoodturnersguild.com

Association of Woodturners of Great Britain
www.woodturners.co.uk

Association of Polelathe Turners and Greenwood Workers
www.bodgers.org.uk

National Association of Woodturners New Zealand
www.naw.org.nz

L'Association des Tourneurs sur Bois du Quebec
www.atbq.qc.ca

Israel Association of Woodturners
www.israelwood.org

Association of Woodturners of South Africa
www.awsa.org.za

FURTHER READING

Bidou, Gerard, and Daniel Guilloux. *Woodturning in France.*
    Paris: Éditions Vial, 1998.
An overview of contemporary turning in France at a period when
it was undergoing an explosion of creativity.

Boase, Tony. *Woodturning Masterclass: Artistry Style, Inspiration.*
    Lewes: GMC Publications Ltd., 1995.
Profiles and galleries of the work of influential British turners.

Christensen, Kip W. and Dale L. Nish. *Beneath the Bark: Twenty-five Years
    of Woodturning.* Utah: Woodturning Symposium, Inc., 2004.
A history and review of work shown over 25 years at the
longest-running woodturning symposium in the world.

Cooke, Edward S., Matthew Kangas, and John Perreault. *Expressions
    in Wood: Masterworks from the Wornick Collection.* The Oakland
    Museum of California in conjunction with an exhibition, 1997.
The first in a series of books on woodturning presenting the field
within the context of a private collection.

Darlow, Mike. *Woodturning Design.* Exeter: Melaleuca Press, 2003.
A review of the history and theory behind design in turning.

Hogbin, Stephen. *Wood Turning: The Purpose of the Object*, Sydney:
    John Ferguson Pty. Ltd. and Crafts Council of Australia, 1980.
A ground-breaking volume that introduced the idea of cutting and
rejoining turned work to create new forms.

Leier, Ray, Jan Peters, and Kevin Wallace. *Contemporary Turned Wood:
    New Perspectives in a Rich Tradition.* Lewes: GMC Publications Ltd., 1999.
The first in a new breed of books to present pioneering artists and
newcomers in the field with a minimum of critical analysis.

Meilach, Dona Z. *Wood Art Today.* Atglen: Schiffer Publishing Ltd., 2004.
An international review of the field of wood art, which partly grew out
of the turning revival. Includes the work of many modern masters.

Nish, Dale. *Artistic Woodturning*. Provo: Brigham Young University Press, 1975.

Nish, Dale. *Master Woodturners*. Provo, Artisan Press, 1985.
Nish's books were an early inspiration for many artists.

Raffan, Richard. *Turning Wood*. Newtown: Taunton Press, 2001.
An introduction to the principles and processes of woodturning by one of the most famous turners in the world.

Ramljak, Suzanne, Michael W. Monroe, Mark Richard Leach, and Arthur Mason. *Turning Wood Into Art: The Jane and Arthur Mason Collection*. Harry N. Abrams, 2000.
Turning Wood into Art was presented in conjunction with an exhibition at the Mint Museum of Craft + Design and features pioneering and leading figures in the field of woodturning.

Ullmer, Sean M., David Revere McFadden, Terry Martin, and Janice Blackburn. *Nature Transformed: Wood Art from the Bohlen Collection*. Marquand Books in association with Hudson Hills Press, 2004.

Fike, Bonita, *The Fine Art of Wood: The Bohlen Collection*. Abbeville Press, 2000.
Books on the Bohlen Collection were produced in conjunction with museum exhibitions and introduced a number of new artists, creating critical dialogue regarding the future of the woodturning field.

Wood Turning in North America since 1930. Philadelphia: Wood Turning Center and Yale University Art Gallery, 2001.
A definitive history of the development of the contemporary woodturning movement in the United States.

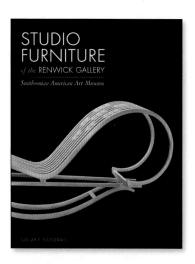
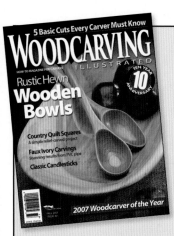
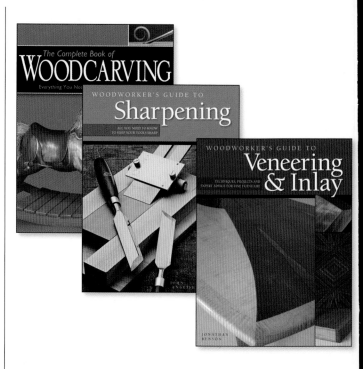

Mike Darlow's Woodturning Series

Fundamentals of Woodturning
By Mike Darlow

From woodturning's premiere instructor, this lavishly illustrated guide is the complete introduction to the craft of creating boxes, bowls, toys and much more on the lathe.

ISBN: 978-1-56523-355-3
$24.95 • 200 pages

"A treasure trove that is essential to anyone who wants to master woodturning…You absolutely have to buy this book."
—Ron Hampton, More Woodturning

Woodturning Methods
By Mike Darlow

The follow-up to the classic beginners guide, *Fundamentals of Woodturning*, this book takes the turner to the next level of projects including spheres, ellipses & other fascinating shapes.

ISBN: 978-1-56523-372-0
$24.95 • 200 pages

Woodturning Chessmen
By Mike Darlow

This complete and fascinating reference details the history, design, and origin of chessmen for woodworkers, woodturners, and chess players.

ISBN: 978-1-56523-373-7
$24.95 • 176 Pages

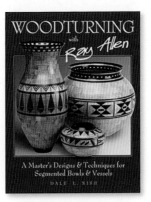

Woodturning with Ray Allen
By Dale Nish
ISBN: 978-1-56523-217-4
$24.95 • 144 pages

Woodturning Jewellery
By Hilary Bowen
ISBN: 978-1-56523-278-5
$22.95 • 160 Pages

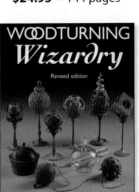

Woodturning Wizardry
By David Springett
ISBN: 978-1-56523-279-2
$27.95 • 192 Pages

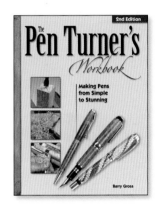

The Pen Turner's Workbook, 2nd Edition
By Barry Gross
ISBN: 978-1-56523-319-5
$14.95 • 136 Pages

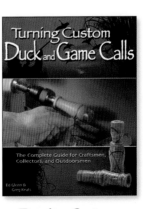

Turning Custom Duck & Game Calls
By Ed Glenn and Greg Keats
ISBN: 978-1-56523-281-5
$19.95 • 128 Pages

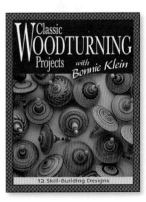

Classic Woodturning Projects with Bonnie Klein
By Bonnie Klein
ISBN: 978-1-56523-260-0
$14.95 • 72 Pages